PYTHON
PROGRAMMING
FOR BEGINNERS

The #1 Python Programming Crash Course
to Learn Python Coding Well And Fast
(with Hands-On Exercises)

2 in 1 Theory and Practice

CODEONE PUBLISHING

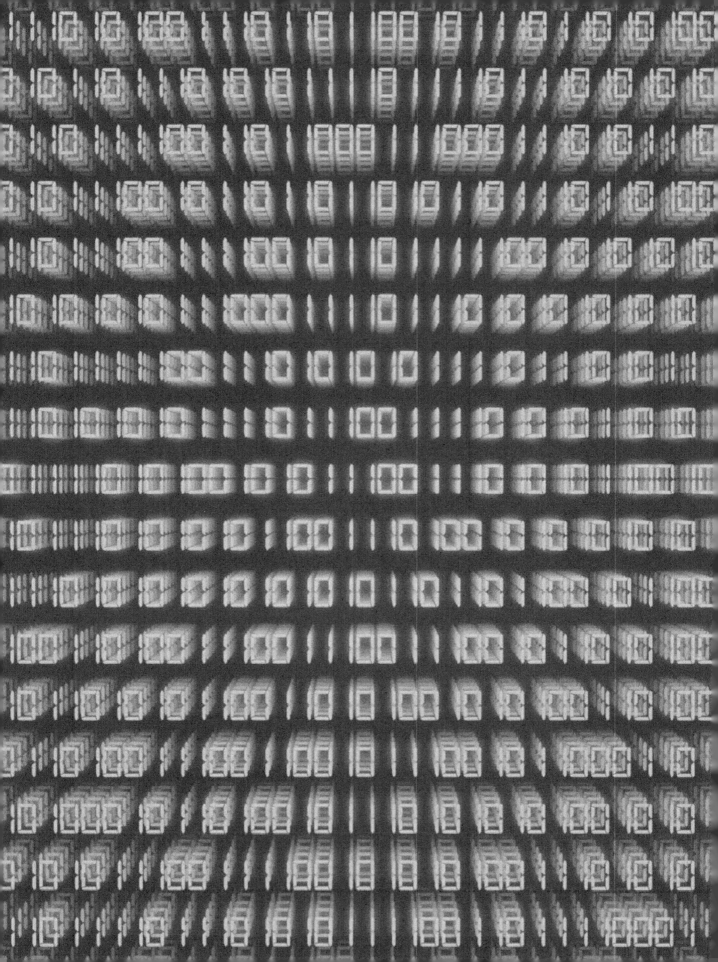

Table of Contents

PART 2 67

PART 1

Intro to Python

This book is about Python for beginners. It introduces the core aspects of the Python programming language. Python is a high-level, integrated, general-purpose programming language developed in 1991 by Guido van Rossum. The design philosophy underpinning Python emphasizes on code readability characterized by its use of considerable whitespace. Python's object-oriented approach and language constructs focus on helping programmers write logical, clear code for large- and small-scale projects. This book aims to provide a cogent introduction to Python for beginners. It seeks to provide a platform to learn Python programming well and in one week including step-by-step practical examples, exercises, and tricks.

Before we go into the "why programming" discussion, let us first define what programming is. Programming is the process of taking an equation and converting it into a code, a programming language, so that it is implemented on a machine. Or in simple words, "Programming is a language to teach a machine what to do through a set of instructions." Various types of programming languages are used, such as the following:

- Python

- PHP

- C language

- JAVA

So why is it important? What's so great about this? Why does it matter?

Almost everything in today's world is done on computers. Whether you're sending an email to a relative, a picture to a friend, or having an important meeting with a colleague on Skype, it has become a necessity for individuals to have access to a computer or laptop. The reliance on computers by individuals and workplaces can be attributed to their speed, reliability, and ease of use. So, when computers are as much a part of life as they are now, learning to program will boost your quality of life! One of the main reasons people are learning programming is because they want to make a career of creating websites for companies or mobile apps. That is not the only reason you need to learn programming; programming can also help improve efficiency and productivity!

What is Python?

Python is a multi-purpose language created by Guido van Rossum. Different from HTML, CSS, and JavaScript, Python can be used for multiple types of programming and software development. Python can be used for things like

- back end software development,
- desktop apps,
- big data and mathematical computations,
- system scripts,
- data analysis,
- data science, or
- Artificial Intelligence.

The reasons why Python is the go-to language for many can be summarized in the following points:

- Beginner friendliness, as it reads almost like English;
- No hard rules on how to build features;
- Easy-to-manage errors;
- Many large, supportive communities;
- Career opportunities; and
- Future, especially for the strong fit towards data science and machine learning applications.

Python is one of the most powerful programming languages. It's one of the programming languages that are interpreted rather than compiled. This means the Python Interpreter, which works line by line, operates on Python programs to give the user the results. With Python, one can do a lot. Python has been used for the development of apps that span a wide of fields, from the most basic apps to the most complex ones. Python can be used for the development of basic desktop computer applications. It is also a good coding language for web development. Websites developed with Python are known for the level of security and protection they provide, making them safe and secure from hackers and other malicious users. Python is well applicable in the field of game development. It has been used for the development of basic and complex computer games. Python is currently the best programming language for use in data science and machine learning. It has libraries that are best suitable for use in data analysis, making it suitable for use in this field. A good example of such a library is scikit-learn (sklearn) which has proved to be the best for use in data science and machine learning.

Python is well known for its easy-to-use syntax. It was written with the goal of making coding easy. This has made it easy the best language even for beginners. Its semantics are also easy, making it easy for one to understand Python codes. The language has received a lot of changes and improvements, especially after the introduction of Python 3. Previously, we had Python 2.7 which had gained much stability. Python 3 brought in new libraries, functions, and other features, and some of the language's construct was changed significantly.

_ *Features of Python*

Python is Easy
Python is an easy language to get started with. The ease of use is underscored by the fact that most of the programs written in Python look similar to the English language. Therefore, this simplicity makes Python an ideal learning language for entry-level programming courses, and thus introducing programming concepts to students.

Python is Portable/Platform Independent
Python is massively portable, which means that Python programs can be run in various operating systems without needing specific or extensive changes.

Python is an Interpreted Language
Mainly, Python is an interpreted language as opposed to being a compiled language. C and C++ are examples of compiled languages.

In many cases, the programs composed in a high-level language are typically referred to as source code or source programs. As a result, the commands in the source codes are referred to as statements. A computer lacks the capacity to execute a program written in high-level language. Typically, computers understand machine language, which comprises of 1s and 0s only.

As a result, there are two types of programs available to users when translating high-level languages to machine languages: compiler and interpreter.

Compiler

In its operative function, a compiler translates the entire source code into the readable machine language in one swoop. The machine language is subsequently executed. The process is illustrated below:

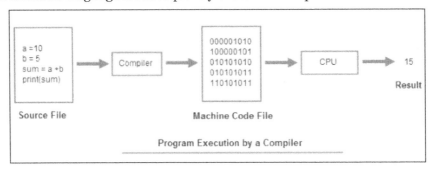

Program Execution by a Compiler

Interpreter

An interpreter employs a line by line approach to translating a high-level language into machine language, which is subsequently executed. The Python interpreter begins at the top of the file, translates the beginning line into machine language, and subsequently executes it. The process repeatedly continues throughout the entire file as illustrated below:

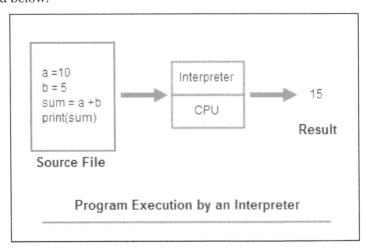

Program Execution by an Interpreter

It is crucial to distinguish between high-level and compiled languages. For example, compiled languages such as C and C++ use a compiler to translate and interpret (high-level to machine language). On the other hand, an interpreted language such as Python employs an interpreter to conduct this approach of translation and subsequent execution. The important distinction here is that compiled language generally operates and performs better compared to written programs that employ interpreted languages. However, Python does not suffer from this disadvantage.

In synthesis, Python is an interpreted language as the program executes directly from the source code. Every time Python programs are run, the source code is required. What Python does is convert the source code written by the developer into an intermediate code which is then further converted into the machine language ready to be executed. Python is processed in real time by the interpreter and the source code does not need to be compiled before its execution. Compiled means that the code needs to be converted to machine language before runtime.

Python is Dynamically Typed

Another characteristic of Python is that it is dynamically typed, which means that data types are checked on the fly during execution, rather than being checked before run time (statically typed).

Python is Strongly Typed

The primary feature of a strongly typed language is that it lacks the capacity to convert one form (type) of data to another automatically. On the other hand, languages such as PHP and JavaScript, which are loosely typed, have the capacity to convert data from one type to another freely and automatically. Consider the following case:

```
1  price = 12
2  str = "The total price = " + 12
3  console.log(str)
```

Output:

```
The total price = 12
```

In this regard, before adding 12 to the string, the JavaScript language seeks to convert the number 12 to a string "12", which is subsequently appended to the end of the string. However, in a Python statement such as below:

```
str = "The total price = " + 12
```

The language (Python) would occasion an error because it does not have the capacity to convert the umber 12 into a string.

In synthesis, Python is a strongly typed language, meaning the type of variables must be known. This implies that the type of a value doesn't change in unexpected ways. For example, a string containing only a number doesn't automatically change into a number, as may happen in Perl. In Python, every data type change needs an explicit conversion.

_ A huge set of libraries

Python provides users with a broad range of libraries, which make it easy to add new capacities and capabilities without necessarily reinventing new approaches. The following sections will go through common questions mostly posed by beginners in Python programming.

_ What type of application can I create using Python?

Some of the main applications for which Python is used include

- games,
- machine learning and Artificial Intelligence,
- data science and data visualization,
- web development,
- game development,
- desktop GUI,
- web scraping applications,
- business applications,
- audio and video applications,
- CAD applications,
- embedded applications,
- system administration applications,
- GUI applications,
- console applications,
- scientific applications, and
- Android applications.

Who uses Python?

Some of the main companies that utilize Python include

- YouTube;
- Mozilla;
- Dropbox;
- Quora;
- Disqus;
- Reddit;
- Google;
- Disney;
- Mozilla;
- Bit Torrent;
- Intel;
- Cisco;
- banks such as JPMorgan Chase, UBS, Getco, and Citadel apply Python for financial market forecasting;
- NASA for scientific programming tasks;
- iRobot for commercial robotic vacuum cleaner;
- and many others.

Chapter 1: Installing Python

To code in Python, you must have the Python Interpreter installed on your computer. You must also have a text editor in which you will be writing and saving your Python codes. The good thing about Python is that it can run on various platforms like Windows, Linux, and Mac OS. Most of the current versions of these operating systems come installed with Python. You can check whether Python has been installed on your operating system by running this command on the terminal or operating system console:
Python

Type the above command on the terminal of your operating system then hit the enter/return key.

The command should return the version of Python installed on your system. If Python is not installed, you will be informed that the command is not recognized; hence you have to install Python.

_ *Choosing a Python Version*

The main two versions of Python are 2.x and 3.x. Python 3.x is the latest one but Python 2.x, as of today, is most likely still the most used version. Python 3.x is however growing much faster in terms of adoption. While Python 2.x is still in use in many software companies, more and more enterprises are moving to Python 3.x. There are several technical differences between the two versions but, put simply, Python 2.x is legacy and Python 3.x is the future. You would be advised to go for the latest version, Python 3.x, as Python 2.x will not be supported after 2020.

_ *General installation instructions*

Installing Python is very easy. All you need to do is follow the steps described below:
1) Go to Python's downloads page: https://www.python.org/downloads/
2) Click the link related to your operating system.

> Looking for Python with a different OS? Python for Windows,
> Linux/UNIX, Mac OS X, Other

3) Click on the latest release and download according to your operating system.
4) Launch the package and follow the installation instructions (we recommend leaving the default settings).
   Make sure you click on Add Python 3.x to PATH. Once the installation is finished you are set to go!

5) Access your terminal IDLE.

Test that all works by writing your first Python code:

```
print ("I'm running my first Python code")
```

Press enter or return, this is what you should get

```
>>> print ("I'm running my first Python code")
I'm running my first Python code
```

You can do the same also by launching this command using a file. We will address this after we address the Python IDLE or another code editor.

_ *Installation on Windows*

To install Python on Windows, download Python from its official website then double-click the downloaded setup package to launch the installation. You can download the package by clicking this link:

https://www.python.org/downloads/windows/

It will be good for you to download and install the latest package of Python as you will be able to enjoy using the latest Python packages. After downloading the package, double-click on it and you will be guided through on-screen instructions on how to install Python on your Windows OS.

_ *Installation on Linux (Ubuntu)*

In Linux, there are a number of package managers that can be used for the installation of Python in various Linux distributions. For example, if you are using Ubuntu Linux, run this command to install Python:

$ sudo apt-get install python3-minimal

Python will be installed on your system. However, most of the latest versions of various Linux distributions come installed with Python. Just run the "python" command. If you get a Python version as the return, then Python has been installed on your system. If not, go ahead and install Python.

_ *Installation on Mac OS*

To install Python in Mac OS, you must first download the package. You can find it by opening the following link on your web browser:

https://www.python.org/downloads/mac-osx/

After the setup has been downloaded, double-click it to launch the installation. You will be presented with on-screen instructions that will guide you through the installation process. Then, you will have Python running on your Mac OS system.

Running Programs

One can run Python programs in two main ways:

- Interactive interpreter
- Script from the command line

Interactive Interpreter or Interactive Mode via Shell

Python comes with a command line, referred to as the interactive interpreter. You can write your Python code directly on this interpreter and press the enter key to get instant results. If you are on Linux, you only have to open the Linux terminal and type "python." Hit the enter key, and the >>> symbol will show on the Python interpreter. To access the interactive Python interpreter on Windows, click Start -> All programs, then identify "Python..." from the list of programs. In my case, I find "Python 3.5" as I have installed Python

3.5. Expand this option and click "Python...." In my case, I click "Python 3.5 (64-bit)" and I get the interactive Python interpreter.

Here, you can write and run your Python scripts directly. To write the "Hello" example, type the following on the interpreter terminal:

```
print("Hello")
```

Hit the enter/return key and the text "Hello" will be printed on the interpreter:

Script from Command Line

This method involves writing Python programs in a file, then invoking the Python interpreter to work on the file. Files with Python should be saved with a .py extension. This is a designation to signify that it is a

Python file. For example, script.py, myscript.py, etc. After writing your code in the file and saving it with the name "mycode.py", you can open the operating system command line and invoke the Python interpreter to work on the file. For example, you can run this command on the command line to execute the code on the file mycode.py:

```
python mycode.py
```

The Python interpreter will work on the file and print the results on the terminal.

Python IDE (Integrated Development Environment)

If you have a GUI (Graphical User Interface) application capable of supporting Python, you can run Python on a GUI environment. The following are the Python IDEs for the various operating systems:

- UNIX—IDLE
- Windows—PythonWin
- Macintosh—IDLE IDE, downloadable from the official website as MacBinary or BinHex'd files.

Chapter 2: IDLE and Python Shell

As we have seen, Python can be used in two main modes:

1) Via Python Shell, also known as the interactive mode
2) Via Python IDLE

As a reminder, the Python Shell known as the prompt string is ready to accept commands. Python Shell allows you to type Python code and receive immediate results and is ideal for testing a small chunk of code. The Python IDLE (Integrated Development and Learning Environment) provides this benefit as well, including additional functionalities. Therefore, we advise you to go straight for the Python IDLE. To start using Python IDLE, we recommend creating a new directory, such as "PythonPractice," where you will save future Python files.

Installing the Interpreter

As a reminder, we have to download the appropriate interpreter for our computers before we can write our first Python program.

We'll be using Python 3 in this book because, as stated on the official Python site, "Python 2.x is legacy; Python 3.x is the present and future of the language." In addition, "Python 3 eliminates many quirks that can unnecessarily trip up beginning programmers." However, note that Python 2 is currently still rather widely used. Python 2 and 3 are about 90% similar. Hence if you learn Python 3, you will likely have no problems understanding codes written in Python 2.

To install the interpreter for Python 3, head over to the following website:
https://www.python.org/downloads/

The correct version should be indicated at the top of the webpage. We'll be using version 3.6.1 in this book. Click to "Download" and the software will start downloading.

Alternatively, if you want to install a different version, scroll down the page and you'll see a listing of other versions. Click on the released version that you want and you'll be redirected to the download page for that version.

Scroll down towards the end of the page and you'll see a table listing various installers for that version. Choose the correct installer for your computer. The installer you should use depends on two factors:
1. The operating system (Windows, Mac OS, or Linux) you are using.
2. The processor (32-bit vs 64-bit) you are using.

For instance, if you are using a 64-bit Windows computer, you will likely be using the "Windows x86-64 executable installer." Just click on the link to download it. If you download and run the wrong installer, no worries. You will get an error message and the interpreter will not install. Simply download the correct installer and you are good to go. Once you have successfully installed the interpreter, you are ready to start coding in Python.

_ Python IDLE

We advise using at least the default Python IDLE. However, there are many other options compared in the table below. IDLE is the integrated development environment (IDE) for Python and it is installed automatically with Python. As well as a neat graphical user interface, IDLE is packed with features that make using Python for developing easy, including a very powerful feature: syntax highlighting.
With syntax highlighting, reserved keywords, literal text, comments, and so on are all highlighted in different colors, making it much easier to see errors in your code. You can both edit and execute your programs in IDLE.

Features	IDLE	Thonny	Eric Python	Atom	Wing	Sublime	Rodeo	PyDev	Spyder	PyCharm
Code Completion	X	✓	✓	✓	✓	✓	✓	✓	✓	✓
Debugging	✓	✓	✓	Package Available	✓	Package Available	X	Remote Debugger	✓	✓
Built-in Unit Testing	X	X	✓	Package Available	✓	Package Available	X	✓	Plugin	✓
Open Source	✓	✓	✓	✓	X	X	✓	✓	✓	Community Edition
Light Weight	✓	✓	X	✓	✓	✓	X	✓	X	X
Refactoring	X	X	X	Package Available	✓	Package Available	X	✓	✓	✓

When you install Python, you get IDLE, an integrated IDE. To start it in Windows, find the ArcGIS folder on your computer. Inside the Python folder, you will see IDLE as a choice—to start IDLE, select it. IDLE has an interactive interpreter built in and can easily run full scripts. The GUI module built into Python is used to write IDLE so it is the same language as the one it will execute.

IDLE has another advantage over python.exe in that script outputs, including print statements, are sent straight to the interactive window in IDLE and don't disappear once the script has been executed. IDLE also uses little memory.

Disadvantages to IDLE can be seen in code assist, such as autocomplete, and the organization in terms of logical projects. Every variable in a script cannot be located like in other IDEs and there is a limit to the number of scripts listed in the Recent Files menu—this is a bit of an obstruction when it comes to finding scripts that haven't been run for a while. IDLE is an ideal IDE to use, however, if there aren't any other options and you need to quickly test a snippet of code.

Using the Python Shell, IDLE and Writing our FIRST program

We'll be writing our code using the IDLE program that comes bundled with our Python interpreter. To do that, let's first launch the IDLE program. You launch the IDLE program like how you launch any other program. For instance, on Windows 10, you can search for it by typing "IDLE" in the search box. Once it is

found, click on IDLE (Python GUI) to launch it. You'll be presented with the Python Shell shown below.

The Python Shell allows us to use Python in interactive mode. This means we can enter one command at a time. The Shell waits for a command from the user, executes it, and returns the result of the execution. After this, the Shell waits for the next command.

Try typing the following into the Shell. The lines starting with >>> are the commands you should type while the lines after the commands show the results. In this book:

Commands = codes inside bordered box

Results = After the symbol "→"

```
2+3
```
  → 5

```
3>2
```
  → True

```
print("Hello World")
```
→ Hello World

When you type 2+3, you are issuing a command to the Shell, asking it to evaluate the value of 2+3. Hence, the Shell returns the answer 5. When you type 3>2, you are asking the Shell if 3 is greater than 2. The Shell replies True. Next, print is a command asking the Shell to display the line Hello World.

_ *Python Interactive Mode*

Python Shell is a very convenient tool for testing Python commands, especially when we are first getting started with the language. However, if you exit from the Python Shell and enter it again, all the commands you type will be gone. Also, you cannot use the Python Shell to create an actual program. To code an actual program, you need to write your code in a text file and save it with a .py extension. This file is known as a Python script.

_ *Python Script Mode*

To create a Python script, click on File > New File in the top menu of our Python Shell. This will bring up the text editor that we are going to use to write our very first program, the "Hello World" program. Writing the "Hello World" program is kind of like the rite of passage for all new programmers. We'll be using this program to familiarize ourselves with the IDLE software.

Type the following code into the text editor (not the Shell).

```
#Prints the Words "Hello World"
print ("Hello World")
```
→ Hello World

You should notice that the first line is in red while, on the second line, the word "print" is in purple and "Hello World" is in green. This is the software's way of making our code easier to read. The words print and "Hello World" serve different purposes in our program, hence they are displayed using different colors. We'll go into more details in later chapters. The line "#Prints the Words "Hello World"" (in red) is actually not part of the program. It is a comment written to make our code more readable for other programmers. This line is ignored by the Python interpreter. To add comments to our program, we type a # sign in front of each line of comment, like this:

```
#This is a comment
#This is also a comment
#This is yet another comment
```

Alternatively, we can also use three single quotes (or three double quotes) for multiline comments, like this:

```
'''
This is a comment
This is also a comment
This is yet another comment
'''
```

Now click File > Save As to save your code. Make sure you save it with the .py extension.

Done? Voilà! You have just successfully written your first Python program.

Finally click on Run > Run Module to execute the program (or press F5). You should see the words "Hello World" printed on your Python Shell.

How to Write a Python Program and Run it in IDLE

1. Start IDLE—open Start > All Programs > Python > IDLE

2. A window with a title of Python Shell will open

3. Click on File > New Window

4. Now a new window called Untitled will load

5. Click on File > Save As and choose a location for your program file

6. Where it says File Name, type program1/py in the box

7. Click on Save

8. A blank window will open—this is an editor window and it is ready for you to type your program in.

9. Type the following statement in exactly as written—it will work on Python 2.x or 3.x:

print ("Hello World")

10. Open the Run menu and click on Run Module to run the program

11. You will now see a message asking you to save your program (it will say Source) so click OK

12. Your program will now run in a Python Shell window

13. To quit Python, shut down all Python windows

Important Note:

If you want to open your file again, find it in the folder you saved it in. Right-click on it and then choose Edit with IDLE from the menu—this will open the editor window.

_Other Python Interactive Developer Environment (IDE)

One of the best IDEs to use with Python is Eclipse so, if you wish, you can install it on your computer.

1. Go to http://www.eclipse.org/downloads and download the Eclipse installation.
2. Proceed with installation
3. To start Eclipse, go to the installation directory and double-click on eclipse.exe.

_The Eclipse Python Plugin

PyDev is an Eclipse Python IDE and it can be used in several different Python distributions. It supports graphical debugging, code refactoring, code analysis, and lots more besides. PyDev can be installed through the Eclipse update manager by going to http://pydev.org/updates. Just check the box beside PyDev and follow the on-screen instructions to install it.

Next, you need to configure Eclipse so it knows where Python is.

1. Open Window > Preferences
2. Click on the option for PyDev and then click on Interpreter Python
3. Click New Configuration
4. Add the executable path for Python

Eclipse IDE is now set up on your computer and ready to use with Python.

_Types of Errors

Three main types of errors can be encountered when programming in Python 3:

- Syntax Errors
- Runtime Errors
- Logical Errors

Syntax Errors

The syntax is a set of guidelines that need to be followed to write correctly in a computer language. A syntax error is a missing punctuation character, a mistake such as a misspelled keyword, or a missing closing bracket. The syntax errors are detected by the compiler or the interpreter. If you try to execute a Python program that contains a syntax error, you will get an error message on your screen and the program won't execute. You must correct any errors and then try to execute the program again. Usually these types of errors are due to typos. In the case an error occurs, the Python interpreter stops running. Some common causes of syntax errors are due to

- wrongly written keywords,
- wrong use of an operator,
- forgetting parentheses in a function call, or
- not putting strings in single quotes or double quotes.

Runtime Errors

These errors occur when the execution of the code is stopped because of an operation being impossible to be carried out. A runtime error can cause a program to end abruptly or even cause a system shutdown. Such errors can be the most difficult errors to detect. Running out of memory or a division by zero are examples of runtime errors.

Logical Errors

Logical errors happen when the code produces wrong results. For instance, a temperature conversion from Fahrenheit to Celsius:

```
print("20 degree Fahrenheit in degree Celsius is: ")
print(5 / 9 * 20 - 32)
```

Result

$\rightarrow$ 1	$\rightarrow$	20 degree Fahrenheit in degree Celsius is:
$\rightarrow$ 2	$\rightarrow$	-20.88888888888889

The above code outputs -20.88888888888889, that is erroneous. The right result is -6.666. These types of errors are referred as logical errors. To get the correct answer, parentheses need to be used correctly: 5 / 9 * (20 - 32) instead of 5 / 9 * 20 - 32.

A logical error is an error that prevents your program from doing what you expected it to do. With logical errors, you get no warning at all. Your code compiles and runs but the result is not the expected one. You must review your program thoroughly to find out where your error is. Python program executes as normal. It is the programmer who has to find and correct the erroneously written Python statement, not the computer or the interpreter. Computers may not be that smart after all.

Chapter 3: Data Types and Variables in Python

Every program has certain data that allow it to function and operate in the way we want. The data can be a text, a number, or any other thing in between. Whether complex or simple, these data types are the cogs in a machine that allow the rest of the mechanism to connect and work. Python is a host to a few data types and, unlike its competitors; it does not deal with an extensive range of things.

That is good because we have less to worry about and yet achieve accurate results despite the lapse. Python was created to make our lives, as programmers, a lot easier.

_ *Strings*

In Python and other programming languages, any text values, such as names, places, or sentences, are referred to as strings. A string is a collection of characters, not words or letters, marked by the use of single or double quotation marks. To display a string, use the print command, open up a parenthesis, put in a quotation mark, and write anything.

Once done, we generally end the quotation marks and close the bracket. If you are using PyCharm, IntelliSense detects what we are about to do and delivers the rest for us immediately. You may have noticed how it jumped to the rescue when you only type in the opening bracket. It will automatically provide you with a closing one. Similarly, when you insert quotation marks, it will provide the closing ones for you.

See why we are using PyCharm?

It greatly helps us out. "I do have a question. Why do we use either single or double quotation marks if both provide the same result?" Ah! Quite an eye.

There is a reason we use different quotation marks. Let me explain by using the example below:

print('I'm afraid I won't be able to make it')
print("He said "Why do you care?"")

Try to run this through PyCharm. To run, simply click on the green play-like button on the top right side of the interface.

> "C:\Users\Programmer\AppData\Local\Programs\Python\Python37-32\python.exe" "C:/Users/Programmer/PycharmProjects/PFB/Test1.py"

> File "C:/Users/Programmer/PycharmProjects/PFB/Test1.py", line 1

```
print('I'm afraid I won't be able to make it')
```

→ SyntaxError: invalid syntax

Process finished with exit code 1

Here's a hint: That's an error!

So what happened here? Try and revisit the inputs. See how we started the first print statement with a single quote? Immediately, we ended the quote using another quotation mark. The program only accepted the letter "I" as a string.

You may have noticed how the color may have changed for every other character from "m" until "won," after which the program detects yet another quotation mark and accepts the rest as another string. Quite confusing, to be honest.

Similarly, in the second statement, the same thing happened. The program saw double quotes and understood it as a string, right until the point the second instance of double quotation marks arrives. That's where it did not bother checking whether it is a sentence or that it may have still been going on. Computers do not understand English; they understand binary communications. The compiler is what runs when we press the run button. It compiles our code and interprets the same into a series of ones and zeros so that the computer may understand what we are asking it to do.

This is exactly why the second it spots the first quotation mark, it considers it as a start of a string, and ends it immediately when it spots a second quotation mark, even if the sentence was carrying onwards. To overcome this obstacle, we use a mixture of single and double quotes when we know we need to use one of these within the sentence. Try to replace the opening and closing quotation marks in the first state as double quotation marks on both ends. Likewise, change the quotation marks for the second statement to single quotation marks as shown here:

```
print("I'm afraid I won't be able to make it")
print('He said "Why do you care?"')
```

Now the output should look like this:

→ I'm afraid I won't be able to make it

→ He said, "Why do you care?"

Lastly, for strings, the naming convention does not apply to the text of the string itself. You can use regular English writing methods and conventions without worries, as long as that is within the quotation marks. Anything outside it will not be a string in the first place, and will not or may not work if you change the cases.

Numeric Data type

Python is able to recognize numbers rather well. The numbers are divided into two pairs:

- Integer—A positive and/or negative whole number that is represented without any decimal points.
- Float—A real number that has a decimal point representation.

This means, if you were to use 100 and 100.00, one would be identified as an integer while the other will be deemed a *float*. So why do we need to use two number representations?

Suppose you are designing a small game that has a character's life of 10. You might wish to write the program in a way that whenever a character takes a hit, his life reduces by one or two points. However, to make things a little more precise, you may need to use float numbers. Now, each hit might vary and may take 1.5, 2.1, or 1.8 points away from the life total. Using floats allows us to use greater precision, especially when calculations are on the cards. If you aren't too troubled about the accuracy, or your programming involves whole numbers only, stick to integers.

_Booleans in Python

Ah! The one with the funny name. Boolean (or bool) is a data type that can only operate on and return two values: True or False. Booleans are a vital part of any program, except the ones where you may never need them, such as our first program. These are what allow programs to take various paths if the result is true or false.

Here's a little example. Suppose you are traveling to a country you have never been to. There are two choices you are most likely to face. If it is cold, you will be packing your winter clothes. If it is warm, you will be packing clothes that are appropriate for warm weather. Simple, right? That is exactly how the Booleans work. We will look into the coding aspect of it as well. For now, just remember, when it comes to true and false, you are dealing with a bool value.

_List Python

While this is slightly more advanced for someone at this stage of learning, the list is a data type that does what it sounds like. It lists objects, values, or stores data within square brackets ([]). Here's what a list would look like:

```
month = ['Jan', 'Feb', 'March', 'And so on!']
month
```

> → ['Jan', 'Feb', 'March', 'And so on!']

We will be looking into this separately, where we will discuss lists, tuples, and dictionaries. We will look at this data type more in detail ahead.

_Variables

If you have the passengers but you do not have a mode of commuting, they will have nowhere to go. These passengers would just be folks standing around, waiting for some kind of transportation to pick them up. Similarly, data types cannot function alone. They need to be "stored" in these vehicles. These special vehicles, what programmers refer to as containers, are called variables, and they are the elements that perform the magic for us.

Variables are specialized containers that store a specific value in them and can then be accessed, called, modified, or even removed when the need arises. Every variable that you create will hold a specific type of data in them. You cannot add more than one type of data within a variable. In other programming languages, you will find that to create a variable, you need to use the keyword "var" followed by an equals mark "=" and then the value.

In Python, it is a lot easier, as shown below:

```
name = "John"
age = 33
weight = 131.50
is_married = True
```

In the above, we have created a variable named "name" and given it a value of characters. If you recall strings, we have used double quotation marks to let the program know that this is a string. We then created a variable called age. Here, we simply wrote 33, which is an integer as there are no decimal figures following that. You do not need to use quotation marks here at all. Next, we created a variable "weight" and assigned a float value to it. Finally, we created a variable called "is_married" and assigned it a "True" bool value. If you were to change the "T" to "t," the system will not recognize it as a bool and will end up giving an error. Focus on how we used the naming convention for the last variable. We will be ensuring that our variables follow the same naming convention.

You can even create blank variables if you feel like you may need these at a later point in time, or wish to initiate them at no value at the start of the application. For variables with numeric values, you can create a variable with a name of your choosing and assign it a value of zero. Alternatively, you can create an empty string as well by using opening and closing quotation marks only.

```
empty_variable1 = 0
empty_variable2 = ""
```

You do not have to necessarily name them like this; you can come up with more meaningful names so that you and any other programmer who may read your code would understand. I have given them these names to ensure anyone can immediately understand their purpose. Now we have learned how to create variables, let's learn how to call them. What's the point of having these variables if we are never going to use them, right? Let's create a new set of variables.

Have a look here:

```
name = "James"
age = 43
height_in_cm = 163
occupation = "Programmer"
```

I do encourage you to use your own values and play around with variables if you like.
In order for us to call the name variable, we simply need to type the name of the variable.
In order to print that to the console, we will do this:

```
print(name)
```

→ James

The same goes for the age, height, and occupation variables. But what if we wanted to print them together and not separately? Try running the code below and see what happens:

```
print(name age height_in_cm occupation)
```

→ SyntaxError: invalid syntax

Surprised? Did you end up with this? Here is the reason that happened. When you were using a single variable, the program knew what variable that was. The minute you added a second, a third, and a fourth variable, it tried to look for something that was written in that manner. Since there wasn't anything, it returned with an error that otherwise says: "Umm... Are you sure? I tried looking everywhere, but I couldn't find this 'name age height_in_cm occupation' element anywhere." All you need to do is add a comma to act as a separator like so:

```
print(name, age, height_in_cm, occupation)
```

→ James 43 163 Programmer

And now it knew what we were talking about. The system recalled these variables and was successfully able to show us what their values were. But what happens if you try to add two strings together? What if you wish to merge two separate strings and create a third string as a result?

```
first_name = "John"
last_name = "Wick"
```

To join these two strings into one, we can use the + sign. The resulting string will now be called a String Object, and since this is Python we are dealing with, everything within this language is considered as an object, thus the Object-Oriented Programming (OOP) nature.

```
first_name = "John"
last_name = "Wick"
first_name + last_name
```

Here, we did not ask the program to print the two strings. If you wish to print these two instead, simply add the print function and type in the string variables with a + sign in the middle within parentheses. Sounds good, but the result will not be quite what you expect:

```
first_name = "John"
last_name = "Wick"
print(first_name + last_name)
```
→ JohnWick

Hmm. Why do you think that happened? Certainly, we did use a space between the two variables. The problem is that the two strings have combined together, quite literally here, and we did not provide a white space (blank space) after John or before Wick; it will not include that. Even the white space can be a part of a string.

To test it out, add one character of space within the first line of code by tapping on the friendly spacebar after John. Now try running the same command again, and you should see "John Wick" as your result. The process of merging two strings is called concatenation. While you can concatenate as many strings as you like, you cannot concatenate a string and an integer together.

If you really need to do that, you will need to use another technique to convert the integer into a string first and then concatenate the same. To convert an integer, we use the str() function.

```
text1 = "Zero is equal to"
text2 = 0
print(text1 + str(text2))
```
→ Zero is equal to 0

Python reads the codes in a line-by-line method. First, it will read the first line, then the second, then third, and so on. This means we can do a few things beforehand as well, to save some time for ourselves.

```
text1 = "Zero is still equal to "
text2 = str(0)
print(text1 + text2)
```
→ Zero is still equal to 0

You may wish to remember this as we will be re-visiting the conversion of values into strings a lot sooner than you might expect. There is one more way through which you can print out both string variables and numeric variables, all at the same time, without the need for + signs or conversion. This way is called String Formatting. To create a formatted string, we follow a simple process as shown here:

```
print(f"This is where {var 1} will be. Then {var 2}, then {var 3} and
so on")
```

Var 1, 2, and 3 are variables.

You can have as many as you like here. Notice the importance of whitespace. Try not to use the spacebar as much. You might struggle at the start but will eventually get the hang of it. When we start the string, we place the character "f" to let Python know that this is a formatted string. Here, the curly brackets are performing a part of placeholders. Within these curly brackets, you can recall your variables. One set of curly brackets will be a placeholder for each variable that you would like to call upon. To put this in practical terms, let's look at an example:

```
show = "GOT"
name1 = "Daenerys"
name2 = "Jon"
name3 = "Tyrion"
seasons = 8
print(f"The show called {show} had characters like {name1},{name2}, and
{name3} in all {seasons} seasons.")
```

→ The show called GOT had characters like Daenerys, Jon, and Tyrion in all 8 seasons.

If you get an error, please make sure you have the latest version of Python installed.

While there are other variations to convert integers into strings and concatenate strings together, it is best to learn those which are used throughout the industry as standard. Now, you have seen how to create a variable, recall it, and concatenate the same. Everything sounds perfect, except for one thing: These are predefined values. What if we need input directly from the end-user? How can we possibly know that? Even if we do, where do we store them?

_ *User-Input Values*

Suppose we are trying to create an online form. This form will contain simple questions like asking for the user's name, age, city, email address, and so on. There must be some way through which we can allow users to input these values on their own and for us to get those back.

We can use the same to print out a message that thanks the users for using the form and that they will be contacted at their email address for further steps. To do that, we will use the input() function. The input function can accept any kind of input. To use this function, we will need to provide it with some reference so that the end-user is able to know what they are about to fill out. Let us look at a typical example and see how such a form can be created:

```
print("Hello and welcome to my interactive tutorial.")
name = input("Your Name: ")
age = int(input("Your age: "))
city = input("Where do you live? ")
email = input("Please enter your email address: ")
print(f"Thank you very much {name}, you will be contacted at {email}.")
```

→ Hello and welcome to my interactive tutorial.

→ Your Name: Sam

→ Your age: 28

→ Where do You live? London

→ Please enter your email address: sam@something.com

→ Thank you very much Sam, you will be contacted at sam@something.com.

In the above, we began by printing a greeting to the user and welcoming them to the tutorial. Next, we created a variable named "name" and assigned it a value that our user will generously provide us with. In the age, you may have noticed I changed the input to int(), just as we changed integer to string earlier on. This is because our message within the input parameters is a string value by default, as it is within quotation marks. You will always need to ensure you know what type of value you are after and do the needful, as shown above. Next, we asked for the name of the city and the email address. Now, using a formatted string, we printed out our final message. "Wait! How can we print out something we have yet to receive or know?" I did mention that Python works line by line. The program will start with a greeting, as shown in the output. Then, it will move to the next line and realize that it must wait for the user to input something and hit enter. This is why the input value has been highlighted by bold and italic fonts here. The program then moves to the next line and waits yet again for the user to put something in and press enter, and this goes on until the final input command is sorted. Now that the program has the values stored, it immediately recalls these values and prints them out for the viewer to see in the end. The result was rather pleasing as it gave a personalized message to the user, and we received the information we need.

Everybody walks away happy! Storing information directly from the user is both essential and, at times, necessary. Imagine a game that is based on Python. The game is rather simple, where a ball will jump when you tap the screen. The problem is, your screen isn't responding to the touch at all for some reason. While that happens, the program will either keep the ball running until input is detected or it will just not work at all. We also use input functions to gather information such as login ID and passwords to match with the database, but that is a point we shall discuss later when we talk about statements. It is a little more complicated than it sounds at the moment, but once you understand how to use statements, you will be one step closer than ever before to becoming a programmer.

Chapter 4: Numbers in Python

We have briefly looked at numbers in the Data Types chapter. In this chapter, we will go into greater detail on how to use and manipulate numbers in Python. Before we go any further, let's have a brief refresher on the different types of numbers available in Python:

- Integer—A whole number without fractions or decimals.

- Floating Point—A number that has a fractional part expressed with a decimal point.

- Complex—A complex number expressed by using a "J" or "j" suffix.

Let's look at a quick example of how these data types can be used.

This program shows how to use number data types in Python:

```
# This program looks at number data types
# An int data type
a=123
# A float data type
b=2.23
# A complex data type
c=3.14J
print(a)
print(b)
print(c)
```

This program's output will be as follows:

→ 123

→ 2.23

→ 3.14j

There are a variety of functions available in Python to work with numbers. Let's look at a summary of them, after which we will look at each in more detail along with a simple example.

Number Functions

Function	Description
abs()	This returns the absolute value of a number
ceil()	This returns the ceiling value of a number
max()	This returns the largest value in a set of numbers
min()	This returns the smallest value in a set of numbers

pow(x,y)	This returns the power of x to y
sqrt()	This returns the square root of a number
random()	This returns a random value
randrange(start,stop,step)	This returns a random value from a particular range
sin(x)	This returns the sine value of a number
cos(x)	This returns the cosine value of a number
tan(x)	This returns the tangent value of a number

_ Abs Function

This function is used to return the absolute value of a number. Let's look at an example of this function.

The following program showcases the abs function.

```
# This program looks at number functions
a=-1.23
print(abs(a))
```

This program's output will be as follows:

→ 1.23

_ Ceil Function

This function is used to return the ceiling value of a number. Let's look at an example of this function. Note that for this program we need to import the "math" module to use the ceil function.

Example: The following program showcases the ceil function.

```
import math
# This program looks at number functions
a=1.23
print(math.ceil(a))
```

This program's output will be as follows:

→ 2

_ Max Function

This function is used to return the largest value in a set of numbers. Let's look at an example of this function.

The program below is used to showcase the max function.

```
# This program looks at number functions
print(max(3,4,5))
```

This program's output will be as follows:

→ 5

Min Function

This function is used to return the smallest value in a set of numbers. Let's look at an example of this function.

The following program shows how the min function works.

```
# This program looks at number functions
print(min(3,4,5))
```

This program's output will be as follows:

→ 3

Pow Function

This function is used to return the value of x to the power of y, where the syntax is "pow(x,y)." Let's look at an example of this function.

The following program showcases the pow function.

```
# This program looks at number functions
print(pow(2,3))
```

This program's output will be as follows:

→ 8

Sqrt Function

This function is used to return the square root of a number. Let's look at an example of this function. Note that for this program we need to import the "math" module in order to use the sqrt function.

The next program shows how the sqrt function works.

```
import math
# This program looks at number functions
print(math.sqrt(9))
```

This program's output will be as follows:

$\rightarrow$ 3.0

Random Function

This function is used to simply return a random value. Let's look at an example of this function.

The following program showcases the random function.

```
import random
# This program looks at number functions
print(random.random())
```

The output will differ depending on the random number generated. Note that for this program we need to use the "random" Python library.
In our case, the program's output is:

$\rightarrow$ 0.0054600853568235691

Randrange Function

This function is used to return a random value from a particular range. Let's look at an example of this function. Note that we again need to import the "random" library for this function to work.

This program is used to showcase the random function.

```
import random
# This program looks at number functions
print(random.randrange(1,10,2))
```

The output will differ depending on the random number generated. In our case, the program's output is:

$\rightarrow$ 5

Sin Function

This function is used to return the sine value of a number. Let's look at an example of this function.

The following program shows how to use the sin function.

```
import math
# This program looks at number functions
print(math.sin(45))
```

This program's output will be as follows:

→ 0.8509035245341184

Cos Function

This function is used to return the cosine value of a number. Let's look at an example of this function.

This program is used to showcase the cos function.

```
import math
# This program looks at number functions
print(math.cos(45))
```

This program's output will be as follows:

→ 0.5253219888177297

Tan Function

This function is used to return the tangent value of a number. Let's look at an example of this function.

The following program shows the use of the tan function.

```
import math
# This program looks at number functions
print(math.tan(45))
```

This program's output will be as follows:

→ 1.6197751905438615

Chapter 5: Operators in Python

1. Arithmetic Operators

These are operators that have the ability to perform mathematical or arithmetic operations that are going to be fundamental or widely used in this programming language, and these operators are in turn subdivided into:

1.1. Sum Operator: Its symbol is (+) and its function is to add the values of numerical data. Its syntax is written as follows:

```
6+4
```
  → 10

1.2 Subtract Operator: Its symbol is (-) and its function is to subtract the values of numerical data types. Its syntax can be written like this:

```
4-3
```
  → 1

1.3 Multiplication Operator: Its symbol is (*) and its function is to multiply the values of numerical data types.
Its syntax can be written like this:

```
3*2
```
  → 6

1.4 Division Operator: Its symbol is (/); the result offered by this operator is a real number. Its syntax is written like this:

```
3.5/2
```
  → 1.75

1.5 Module Operator: Its symbol is (%); its function is to return the rest of the division between the two operators. In the following example, we have the division of 8 by 5, equal to 1 with a remainder of 3. For this reason, its module will be 3.
Its syntax is written like this:

```
8%5
```
→ 3

1.6 Exponent Operator: Its symbol is (**) and its function is to calculate the exponent between numerical data type values. Its syntax is written like this:

```
3**2
```
→ 9

1.7 Whole Division Operator: Its symbol is (//); in this case, the result it returns is only the whole part of the resulting number.
Its syntax is written like this:

```
3.5//2
```
→ 1.0

However, if integer operators are used, the Python language will determine that it wants the result variable to be an integer as well, this way you would have the following:

```
3/2
```
→ 1.5

```
3//2
```
→ 1

If we want to obtain decimals in this particular case, one option is to make one of our numbers real. For example:

```
3.0/2
```
→ 1.5

_ 2. Comparison Operators

Comparison operators are those that will be used to compare values and return the True or False response as a result of the condition applied.

2.1 Operator Equal to: Its symbol is (==); its function is to determine if two values are exactly the same. For example:

```
3==3
```
→ True
```
5==1
```
→ False

2.2 Operator Different than: Its symbol is (!=); its function is to determine if two values are different and, if so, the result will be True. For example:

```
3!=4
```
→ True

```
3!=3
```
→ False

2.3 Operator Greater than: Its symbol is (>); its function is to determine if the value on the left is greater than the value on the right and, if so, the result it yields is True. For example:

```
5>3
```
→ True

```
3>8
```
→ False

2.4 Operator Less than: Its symbol is (<); its function is to determine if the left value is less than the right one and, if so, it gives True as the result. For example:

```
3<5
```
→ True

```
8<3
```
→ False

2.5 Operator Greater than or Equal to: Expressed as (>=), its function is to determine if the value on the left is greater than or equal to the value on the right. If so, the result returned is True. For example:

```
8>=1
```
→ True

```
8>=8
```
→ True

```
3>=8
```
→ False

2.6 Operator Less than or Equal to: Expressed as (<=), its function is to evaluate if the value on its left is less than or equal to the one on the right. If so, the result returned is True. For example:

```
8<=10
```
→ True

```
8<=8
```
→ True

```
10<=8
```
→ False

3. Logical Operators

Logical operators are *and*, *or*, and *not*. Their main function is to check if two or more operators are true or false and, as a result, return a True or False. This type of operator is commonly used in conditionals to return a Boolean by comparing several elements.

In Python, the storage of true and false values are of the bool type, which was named thus by the British mathematician George Boole, who created Boolean algebra. There are only two Boolean values, True and False, and it is important to capitalize them because, in lower cases, they are not Boolean but simple phrases.

The semantics or meaning of these operators is similar to their English meaning, for example, if we have the following expression:

X > 0 and x < 8, this will be true if indeed x is greater than zero and less than 8.

In the case of "or," we have the following example:

```
N=12
N%6==0 or n%8==0
```

   → True

It will be true if any of the conditions are indeed true, that is, if n is a number divisible by 6 or by 8.

The logical operator "not" denies a Boolean expression. So, for example:
not (x < y) will be true if x < y is false, that is, if x is greater than y.

Chapter 6: Strings Methods in Python

There will almost certainly be times where you need to manipulate strings. Maybe you'll need to get its length, or you'll need to split it or make another string from it. Maybe you'll need to read what character is at x position. Whatever the reason is, the point is that there's a way.

This opens us up to a broader discussion on the nature of objects that we're going to go into more in depth later on. In the meantime, we're also going to be covering extremely useful methods that the Python language provides to be used with strings.

Go ahead and create a new file. You can call it whatever you want. My file is going to be named strings.py. Uncreative name, sure, but we're going to be getting creative with strings in this chapter, believe me.

So what is a string, really? Well, we know that a string is a line of text, but what goes into that?

We've spoken quite a bit so far about lists. Lists are a form of another variable used in Python programming called an array. In the most basic terms, an array is a pre-allocated set of data that goes together.

Python comes from and is built upon a language called C. Like in Python, C has data types. Python saves the user time by setting the data type for the programmer instead of having the programmer declare it.

One of the data types in C was called a char, which was a single character. In terms of computer-speak, there isn't native support for strings. Strings were simply arrays of characters. For example, if one wanted to make a string called "hello," they would have done the following:

```
char hello[6] = { 'h', 'e', 'l', 'l', 'o', '\0' };
```

Python, in its beautiful habit of maximum abstraction, keeps us from these complexities and lets us just declare:

```
hello = "hello"
```

The point is that strings, ultimately, are just sets of data. Like any set of data, they can be manipulated, and there will be times where we need to manipulate them.

The most simple form of string manipulation is the concept of concatenation. Concatenated strings are strings that are put together to form a new string. Concatenation is super easy—you simply use the + sign to literally add the strings together:

```
sentence = "My " + "grandmother " + "baked " + "today."
print(sentence)
```
    → My grandmother baked today.

The first thing to remember when working with string manipulation is that strings, like any set of data, start counting at 0. So the string "backpack" would count like so:

```
backpack
01234567
```

There are a few different things that we can do with this knowledge alone. The first is that we can extract a single letter from it.

Let's say the string "backpack" was stored in a variable called backpack. We could extract the letter "p" from it by typing:

```
letter = backpack[4]
print(letter)
```
→ p

This would extract whatever the character at index 4 was in the string. Here, of course, it's p (start counting from 0, letter b is in position 0).

If we wanted to extract the characters from "b" to "p," we could do the following:

```
substring = backpack[0:4]
print(substring)
```
→ back

This would give the variable substring a string equal to the value of backpack's 0 index to 4 index:

```
backpack
01234567
```

Substring, thus, would have the value of "backpack." Quite the word.
There are a few more things you can do with data sets, and strings specifically, in order to get more specific results:

```
backpack[:4]
```
would give you all characters from the start to index four, like just before.

```
backpack[4:]
```

would give you all characters from index 4 to the end.

```
backpack[:2]
```

would give you the first two characters, while backpack[-2:] would give you the last two characters.

```
backpack[2:]
```

would give you everything but the first two characters, while

```
backpack[:-2]
```

would give you everything aside from the last two characters.

However, it goes beyond this simple kind of arithmetic.

String variables also have built-in functions called methods. Most things in Python—or object-oriented languages in general, really—are forms of things called objects. These are essentially variable types that have entire sets of properties associated with them.

Every single string is an instance of the String class, thus making it a string object. The string class contains definitions for methods that every string object can access, as an instance of the String class.

For example, let's create a bit of a heftier string.

```
tonguetwister = "Peter Piper picked a peck of pickled peppers"
```

The string class has a variety of built-in methods you can utilize in order to work with its objects.

Let's take the split method. If you were to type:

```
splitList = tonguetwister.split(' ')
print(splitList)
```

It would split the sentence at every space, giving you a list of each word. splitList, thus, would look a bit like this:

→ ['Peter', 'Piper ', 'picked ', 'a', 'peck', 'of ', 'pickled', 'peppers']

```
print(splitList[1])
```

would give you the value "Piper."

There's also the count method, which would count the number of a certain character. Typing:

```
p_presence = tonguetwister.lower().count('p')
print(p_presence)
```

You would get the number 9.

There's the replace method, which will replace a given string with another. For example, if you typed:

```
tonguetwister = tonguetwister.replace("peppers", "potatoes")
```

tonguetwister would now have the value of "Peter Piper picked a peck of pickled potatoes."

There's the strip, lstrip, and rstrip methods which take either a given character or whitespace off of both sides of the string. This is really useful when you're trying to parse user input. Unstripped user input can lead to unnecessarily large data sets and even buggy code.

The last major one is the join method, which will put a certain character between every character in the string.

```
print("-".join(tonguetwister))
```
    → "P-e-t-e-r- -P-i-p-e-r- -p-i-c-k-e-[...]"

There are also various boolean expressions that will return true or false. The startswith(character) and endswith(character) methods are two fantastic examples. If you were to type:

```
tonguetwister.startswith("P")
```

It would ultimately return true. However, if you were to type instead:

```
tonguetwister.startswith("H")
```

It would ultimately return false. These are used for internal evaluation of strings as well as for evaluating user input.

String.isalnum() will see if all characters in the string are alphanumeric or if there are special characters; string.isalpha() will see if all characters in the string are alphabetic; string.isdigit() will check to see if the string is a digit or not; and string.isspace() will determine if the string is a space or not.
These are all extremely useful for parsing a given string and making determinations on what to do if the string is or isn't a certain way.

Chapter 7: Program Flow Control and If-else, elif Statements in Python

Comparison operators are special operators in Python programming language that evaluate to either True or False. Program flow control refers to a way in which a programmer explicitly specifies the order of execution of program code lines. Normally, flow control involves placing some condition(s) on the program code lines. The most basic form of these conditional statements is the *if statement*. This one is going to provide us with some problems right from the beginning, but knowing a bit about it will help us get the *if else* and other control statements to work the way that we want.

To start, the if statement is going to take the input of the user, and compare it to the condition that you set. If the condition is met here, then the code will continue on, usually showing some kind of message that you set up in the code.

However, if the input does not match up with the condition that you set, the returned value will be False.

If ... else Flow Control Statements

The "if...else" statement will execute the body of if in the case that the test condition is True. Should the if...else test expression evaluate to False, the body of the else will be executed. Program blocks are denoted by indentation. The if...else provides more maneuverability when placing conditions on the code. The if...else syntax can be seen below:

```
if test condition:
    Statements
else:
    Statements
```

Let's make a program that checks whether a number is positive or negative.
Start IDLE.
Navigate to the File menu and click New Window.
Type the following:

```
number_mine=-56
if(number_mine<0):
    print(number_mine, "The number is negative")
else:
    print(number_mine, "The number is a positive number")
```

Assignment

Write a Python program that uses if..else statements to perform the following:
a. Given number=9, write a program that tests and displays whether the number is even or odd.
b. Given marks=76, write a program that tests and displays whether the marks are above pass mark or not, bearing in mind that pass mark is 50.
c. Given number=78, write a program that tests and displays whether the number is even or odd.
d. Given marks=27, write a program that tests and displays whether the marks are above pass mark or not, bearing in mind that pass mark is 50.

Assignment

Write a program that accepts age input from the user, explicitly converts the age into integer data types, then uses if...else flow control to test whether or not the person is under the legal age of 21. Include comments and indentation to improve the readability of the program.

Other follow up work: Write programs in Python using if statement only to perform the following:
1. Given number=7, write a program to test and display only even numbers.

2. Given number1=8 and number2=13, write a program to only display if the sum is less than 10.

3. Given count_int=57, write a program that tests and displays the number if the count is more than 45.

4. Given marks=34, write a program that tests if the marks are less than 50 and, if so, displays the message, "the score is below average."

5. Given marks=78, write a program that tests if the marks are more than 50 and displays the message, "great performance."

6. Given number=21, write a program that tests if the number is an odd number and displays the message, "Yes it is an odd number."

7. Given number=24, write a program that tests and displays if the number is even.

Incidental Using the If Statement

There are many things that you can do with values and variables, but the ability to compare them is something that will make it much easier for you to try to use Python. It is something that people will be able to do no matter what types of values that they have, and they can make sure that they are doing it in the right way so that their program will appear to be as smooth running as possible.

Comparing your variables is one of the many options that Python offers you, and the best way to do it is through an "if statement."

Now, you can create a new file. Below is what you will need to be able to do. Do not forget indentation! Here is the way an incidental will look:

```
apples=6
bus="yellow"
if apples == 0:
    print ("Where are the apples?")
else:
    print ("Did you know that busses are %s?" %bus)
```

Run the code through your Python program. It will look like this.

→ Did you know that busses are yellow?

The easiest way to understand why the output looked like this is because the apples were not included with the variation. There were not zero apples, and that was something that created a problem with the code. For that reason, it wasn't put in the output because there was no way to do it and no way to make it look again.

To make sure that you are going to be able to use it with a not statement, you can use another if statement in combination with that not.

```
if not apples == 0:
```

Now, you can try to run the code again through the program that you created.

Both of the things that you wrote in the code are included with the statements, and then, you will be able to try different things. If you do not want to write out the not statement, you can simply use "!":

```
apples=5
if apples!= 0:
    print("How about apples!")
```

When there is an input in your program, such as the number of apples that someone wants or a fact that they have that they can teach you about, the output will look the same. Either they will get a statement about the apples, or they will get a statement about the bus being yellow. If there are no apples that are put into the equation, then you will have the output show up as "Where are the apples?"

The conditionals you use are made up of simple expressions. When you break them down into even smaller pieces, it is easy to understand how they can be used and what you will be able to do with the expressions that you have. It will also give you the chance to show that there is so much more than what you initially had with the variables and values.

if...elif...else Flow Control Statement in Python

Now think of scenarios where we need to evaluate multiple conditions, not just one or two, but three and more. Think of where you have to choose team members: If not Richard, then Mercy; if not Richard and Mercy, then Brian; if not Richard, Mercy, and Brian, then Yvonne. Real-life scenarios may involve several choices or conditions that have to be captured when writing a program.

Remember that the elif simply refers to "else if" and is intended to allow for checking multiple expressions. The if the block is evaluated first, then the elif block(s), before the else block. In this case, the else block is more of a fallback option when all other conditions return false. Importantly, despite several blocks available in if...elif...else, only one block will be executed. Below shows if...elif...else syntax:

```
if test expression:
    Body of if
elif test expression:
    Body of elif
else:
    Body of else
```

Example

Three conditions are covered in this example, but only one can execute at a given instance.
Start IDLE.
Navigate to the File menu and click New Window.
Type the following:

```
nNum = 1
if nNum == 0:
    print("Number is zero.")
elif nNum > 0:
    print("Number is a positive.")
else:
    print("Number is a negative.")
```

Nested if Statements in Python

Sometimes a condition exists but there are more sub-conditions that need to be covered. This leads to a concept known as nesting. The amount of statements you are able to nest is not limited but you should exercise caution as you will realize nesting can lead to user errors when writing code. Nesting can also complicate maintaining of code. Only indentation can help determine the level of nesting.

Example

Start IDLE.
Navigate to the File menu and click New Window.
Type the following:

```
my_charact=str(input("Type a character here either 'a', 'b' or 'c':"))
if (my_charact != None):
    if (my_charact == 'a'):
        print("a")
    elif (my_charact == 'b'):
        print("b")
    else:
        print("c")
```

Assignment

Write a program that uses the if...else flow control statement to check if it is a non-leap year and display either scenario. Include comments and indentation to enhance the readability of the program.

_ *Absolutes*

There is a way to create conditionals with a block of code that will show you whether or not there is a working conditional, even if it is not true and cannot be verified.
Absolute conditionals come into play when you need to see whether or not you can put in different inputs.
Create the variable

apples

Now, you will need to input the different things that you have created in a version of the file that you saved.

```
print("What is your age?")
age = input()
```

This code will let you see how old someone is. But how exactly does that relate to the number of apples you have?
It doesn't; it just shows you how the variable works so that people can enter age values.
You'll create:

```
apples = input("What number of apples are there?/n")
```

That is the easiest part, and will help you create the variable that you need for the rest of the program:

```
if apples == 1:
    print("I don't know what to do with just one apple!")
```

You'll get an error, though, because apples is just a string and you need to make it an integer. Simple:

```
int(string)
```

Now it will look like this:

```
apples = input("What number of apples are there?/n")
apples = int(apples)
if apples == 1:
    print("I don't know what to do with just one apple!")
```

Put this whole string into your file, or practice changing the wording so you can figure out what you want to do with it. When you have put it in, run it through.

The code will work because you created a variable, you added different elements to it, and you allowed for the input of the "apples" in the sequence so that you would be able to show how things worked with it.

This example allowed you to try new things so that you were doing more with what you learned. While you are creating strings of integers, you will need to make sure that you are transforming them into integers instead of simple strings so that you can make sure that they show up and there are no error codes.

Chapter 8: Loops in Python

Before proceeding into loops, let's review the *if statement*. The Python program first evaluates the test expression, and will execute the statement(s) if the expression is True. The program will not execute the statement(s) if the test expression is False. By convention, the body of it is marked by indentation while the first line is not indented line.

_ *For Loop in Python*

Indentation is used to separate the body of for loop in Python.

Note: Remember that a simple linear list takes the following syntax:

```
Variable_name=[values separated by a comma]
```

Example

Start IDLE.
Navigate to the File menu and click New Window.
Type the following:

```
numbers=[12,3,18,10,7,2,3,6,1] #Variable name storing the list
sum=0 #Initialize sum before usage, very important
for i in numbers: #Iterate over the list
    sum=sum+i
    print("The sum is" ,sum)
```

Assignment

Start IDLE.
Navigate to the File menu and click New Window.
Type the following:
Write a Python program that uses the for loop to sum the following lists.

→ a. marks=[3, 8,19, 6,18,29,15]
→ b. ages=[12,17,14,18,11,10,16]
→ c. mileage=[15,67,89,123,76,83]
→ d. cups=[7,10,3,5,8,16,13]

range() function in Python

The range function (range()) in Python can help generate numbers. Remember that in programming, the first item is indexed 0.

Therefore, range(11) will generate numbers from 0 to 10.

Example

Start IDLE.
Navigate to the File menu and click New Window.
Type the following:

```
print(range(7))
```

The output will be 0,1,2,3,4,5,6

Assignment

Without writing and running a Python program, what will be the output for:

    a.   range(16)
    b.   range(8)
    c.   range(4)

Assignment

Create a program in Python to iterate through the following list and include the message "I listen to (each of the music genres)". Use the for loop, len(), and range(). Refer to the previous example on syntax.

```
folders=['Rumba', 'House', 'Rock']
```

Using For Loop with Else

It is possible to include a for loop with else as an option. The else block will be executed if the items contained in the sequence are exhausted.

Example

Start IDLE.
Navigate to the File menu and click New Window.

Type the following:

```
marks=[12, 15, 17]
for i in marks:
    print(i)
else:
    print("No items left")
```

Assignment

Write a Python program that prints all prime numbers between 1 and 50.

While Loop in Python

In Python, the while loop is used to iterate over a block of program code as long as the test condition stays True. The while loop is used in contexts where the user does not know the number of loop cycles that are required; the while loop body is determined through indentation.

Example

Start IDLE.
Navigate to the File menu and click New Window.
Type the following:

```
i=0
while i<6:
    if i==5:
        break
    else:
        print("inside else")
        i=i+1
```

Assignment

a.   Write a Python program that utilizes the while flow control statement to display the sum of all odd numbers from 1 to 10.

b.   Write a Python program that employs the while flow control statement to display the sum of all numbers from 11 to 21.

c. Write a Python program that incorporates a while flow control statement to display the sum of all even numbers from 1 to 10.

Using While Loop with Else

If the condition is false and no break occurs, a while loop's else part runs.

Example

Start IDLE.
Navigate to the File menu and click New Window.
Type the following:

```
track = 0
while track<4:
    print("Within the loop")
    track = track+1
else:
    print("Now within the else segment")
```

Python's Break and Continue

Let us use a real-life analogy where we force a stop on iteration before it finishes evaluating. Think of cracking or breaking passwords using a simple dictionary attack. You'll want to loop through all possible character combinations, immediately stopping when you strike the password. Again, think of when recovering accidentally deleted photos using recovery software; you will want the recovery to stop iterating through files immediately when it finds items within the specified range. The break and continue statement in Python works similarly.

Example

Start IDLE.
Navigate to the File menu and click New Window.
Type the following:

```
for tracker in "bring":
    if tracker == "i":
        break
    print(tracker)
print("The End")
```

The output of this program will be:

→ b
→ r
→ The End

_Continue Statement in Python

When the continue statement is used, the interpreter skips the rest of the code inside a loop for the current iteration only and the loop does not terminate. The loop continues with the next iteration.
The syntax of Python's continue statement is as follows:
continue

Start IDLE.
Navigate to the File menu and click New Window.
Type the following:

```
for tracker in "bring":
    if tracker == "i":
        continue
    print(tracker)
print("finished")
```

The output of this program will be:

→ b
→ r
→ n
→ g
→ Finished

This statement can be helpful, for example, if you are running data recovery software and have specified for it to skip word files (.doc, dox extension). The program will have to continue iterating even after skipping word files.

PART 2

Chapter 9: Lists in Python

We have learned quite a lot since we started with this book. We have gone through operators, we learned about various data types, and we also looked at loops and statements. During all of this, we did mention the word "list" and represented these with a square bracket instead of curly or round brackets. This chapter will now explore and explain what exactly lists are. By the end of this chapter, we should be familiarized with the core concepts of these and how they are vital to the programming of any kind.

_ *A Look into What Lists Are*

Let us go ahead and create an imaginary family that comprises Smith, Mary, their daughter Alicia, and their son Elijah. How would we do that? Begin by creating a variable named family as shown below:

```
family = ['Smith', 'Mary', 'Alicia', 'Elijah']
```

Using the [] brackets, we provided the data to this variable. Now, this specific variable holds more than one name within it. This is where lists come to the rescue. Through listing, we can store as many values within a variable as we like. In this case, we can stick to four only.

If you now use the print command to print 'family', you should see the following:

→ ['Smith', 'Mary', 'Alicia', 'Elijah']

The values or names stored within the brackets are called as items. To call on the item or to check what item is stored on a specific index number, you can use the method we had used earlier in strings.

```
print(family[0])
```
→ Smith

Instead of showing "S," the complete name was shown. Similarly, if you use the other functions such as the len() function, it would provide you with the length of the list. In this case, it would should you that there are four items in this list. Let us try that out for ourselves.

```
print(len(family))
```
→ 4

You can use the [x:y] function, where x and y are ranges you can set. This can be helpful if the list you are working on contains hundreds of entries. You can filter out the ones you would like to view. You can jump straight to the end of the list by using [-1] to see the last entry. The combinations are endless.

Here is a little brain-teaser. Suppose we have around 100 numbers in a list. They are not listed chronologically and we do not have time to scroll through each one of them. We need to find out which of these numbers is the highest. How can we do that?

This is where lists, loops, and if statements come together. How? Let us look into it right away:

```
numbers = [312, 1434, 68764, 4627, 84, 470, 9047, 98463, 389, 2]
high = numbers[0]
for number in numbers:
    if number > high:
        high = number
        print(f"The highest number is {high}")
```

→ The highest number is 98463

Time to put our thinking cap on and see what just happened.

We started out by providing some random numbers. One of these was surely the highest. We created a variable and assigned it the first item of the list of numbers as its value. We do not know whether this item holds the highest value.

Moving ahead, we initiated a "for" loop with a loop variable called number. This number would iterate each value from numbers. We used an "if" statement to tell the interpreter that if the loop variable "number" is greater than our current set highest number, "high," it should immediately replace that with the value it holds.

Once the program was run, Python sees we assigned "high" the value of the first item, which is 312. Once the loop and if statement begins, Python analyzes if the first item is greater than the value of the variable "high." Surely, 312 is not greater than 312 itself. The loop does not alter the value and ends. Now, the "for" loop restarts, this time with the second item value. This time around, when the "if" statement is executed, Python sees that our variable has a lower value than the one it is currently working on. 312 is far less than in 1434. Therefore, it executes the code within the statement and replaces the value of our variable to the newly found higher value. This process will continue until all values are cross-checked and finally the largest value is maintained. Then, only the largest value will be printed for us.

2-D Lists

In Python, we have another kind of list that is called the two-dimensional list. If you are someone who is willing to master data sciences or machine learning, you will need to use these quite a lot. The 2-D list is quite a powerful tool. Generally, when it comes to maths, we have what is called matrixes. These are arrays of numbers formed in a rectangular form within large brackets.

Unlike your regular lists, these contain rows and columns of values and data as shown here:

```
matrix = [
[19, 11, 91],
[41, 25, 54],
[86, 28, 21]]
```

In an easier way, imagine this as a list that contains a number of lists inside. As illustrated above, each row is now acting as a separate list. Had this been a regular list, we could have printed a value using the index number. How do you suppose we can have the console print out the value of our first item within the first list?

```
print(matrix[0][0])
```

Using the above, you can now command the interpreter to only print out the first value stored within the first list. The first zero within the first [] tells the interpreter which list to access. Following that is the second bracket set which further directs the search to the index number of the item. In this case, we were aiming to print out 19 and thus, 19 will be our result.

Take a moment and try to print out 25, 21, and 86 separately. If you were able to do this, good job.

You can change the values of the items within the list. If you know the location of the said item, you can use the name of the variable followed by the [x][y] position of the item. Assign a new number by using a single equals-to mark and the value you wish for it to have.

The 2-D lists are normally used for slightly advanced programming where you need to juggle quite a lot of values and data types. However, it is best to keep these in mind as you never know when you may actually need to use them.

List Methods

Somewhere in the start, we learned about something called methods. To start off, let us go back to PyCharm and create our own list of random numbers. Let's use the following number sequence:

```
numbers = [11, 22, 33, 44, 55, 66, 77]
```

We are not going to print this out to our console. Instead, we would like to see what possible methods are available for us to use. In the next line, type the name of the variable followed by the dot operator "." to access the methods.

Let us type the append method:

```
numbers.append(10)
```

The append method allows us to add an entry or a value to the list under the selected variable. Go ahead and add any number of your choice. Done? Now try to print the variable named "numbers" and see what happens.

You should be able to see a number added at the end of the list. Good, but what if you don't wish to add a number at the end? What if you want it to be somewhere close to the start?

To do that, we need a method called insert:

```
numbers.insert()
```

In order for us to execute this properly, we will need to first provide this method with the index position where we wish for the new number to be added. If you wish to add it to the start, use zero, or if you wish to add it to any other index, use that number. Follow this number by a comma and the number itself.

Now, if you print the numbers variable, you should be able to see the new number added exactly where you wanted:

```
numbers.insert(2, 20)
print(numbers)
```

→ [11, 22, 20, 33, 44, 55, 66, 77]

Similarly, you can use a method called remove to delete any number you wish to be removed from the list. When using the remove method, do note that it will only remove the number where it first occurred. It will not remove the same number which might have been repeated later on within the same list as shown here:

```
numbers = [11, 22, 33, 44, 55, 66, 77, 37, 77]
numbers.remove(77)
print(numbers)
```

→ [11, 22, 33, 44, 55, 66, 37, 77]

For any given reason, if you decide you no longer require the list content, you can use the clear command. This command does not require you to pass any object within the parentheses:

```
numbers.clear()
```

Using another method, you can check on the index number of a specific value's first occurrence:

```
numbers.index(44)
```

If you run the above, you will get '3' as a result. Why? The index position of three contains the number 44 in the list we used earlier. If you put in a value that is not within the defined list values, you will end up with an error as shown here:

```
print(numbers.index(120))
```

  → ValueError: 120 is not in list

There is another useful method that helps you quite a lot when you are dealing with a bunch of numbers of other data types. In case you are not too sure and you wish to find out whether a specific number exists within a list, you can use the "in" operator as shown:

```
numbers = [11, 22, 33, 44, 55, 66, 77, 37, 77]
print(43 in numbers)
```

What do you think the result will be? An error? You might be wrong. This is where the result will show "False." This is a boolean value and is indicating that the number we wanted to search for does not exist in our list. If the number did exist, the return boolean value would have been "True."

Let us assume that we have a large number of items in the list and we wish to find out just how many times a specific number is being used or repeated within the said list. There is a way we can command Python to do it for us. This is where you will use the "count" method.

In our own list above, we have two occurrences where the number 77 is used. Let us see how we can use this method to find out both instances:

```
print(numbers.count(77))
```

The result will now state "2" as our result. Go ahead and add random numbers to the list with a few repeating ones. Use the count method to find out the number of occurrences and see how the command works for you. The more you practice, the more you will remember.

Now we have seen how to locate, change, add, clear, and count the items in the list. What if we wish to sort the entire list in ascending or descending order? Can we do that?

With the help of the sort method, you can have that carried out. The sort() method by default will only sort the data into ascending order. If you try and access the method within a print command, the console will show "none" as your return. To do this correctly, always use the sort method before or after the print command. To reverse the order, use the reverse() method. This method, just like the sort() method, does not require you to pass any object within the brackets.

_ *Tuples*

In Python, we use lists to store various values that can be accessed, changed, modified, or removed at will. That certainly might not be the best thing to know if you intend to use data that is essential in nature. To overcome that, there is a kind of list that will store the data for you. After it is stored, however, no additional modification will be carried out, accidentally or intentionally. These are called tuples.

Tuples are a form of list which are very important to know when it comes to Python. Unlike the square bracket representation for lists, these are represented by parentheses ():

```
numbers = (19, 21, 28, 10, 11)
```

Tuples are known as immutable items. This is because of the fact that you cannot mutate or modify them. Let us deliberately try to modify the value to see what happens.

As soon as you type in the dot operator to access append, remove, and other similar methods, you should see this instead:

Tuples simply do not have these options anymore. That is because you are trying to modify a value that is secure and locked by Python. You can try another method to see if you can forcefully change the value by doing this:

```
numbers = (19, 21, 28, 10, 11)
print(numbers)
numbers[0] = 10
```

→ TypeError: 'tuple' object does not support item assignment

See how the error came up? The program cannot carry out this change of value, nor can it append the value in any way.

While you will be working with lists most of the time, tuples come in handy to ensure you store values that you know you don't wish to change accidentally in the future. Think of a shape that you wish to create and maintain throughout the game or website as uniform. You can always call on the values of a tuple and use the values when and where needed.

The only way these values might be changed is if you purposely or unintentionally overwrite them. For example, say you had written the values of a tuple within the code and since moved on hundreds of lines ahead. At this point, you might have forgotten about the earlier values or the fact that you wrote these values previously. You start writing new values by using exactly the same name and start storing new values within them. This is where Python will allow you to overwrite the previously stored values without presenting any errors when you run the program.

The reason this can happen is because Python understands that you may wish for a value to change later on and then stay the same for a while until you need to change them yet again. When you execute the program, the initially stored values will continue to remain in use right up until the point where you want them to be changed. In order to do that, you can simply do the following:

```
numbers = (1, 2, 3, 4, 5)
print(numbers)
```
→ (1, 2, 3, 4, 5)

```
numbers = (6, 7, 8, 9, 10)
print(numbers)
```
→ (6, 7, 8, 9, 10)

The number values have changed without the program screaming back at us with an error. As long as you know and you do this change on purpose, there is absolutely nothing to worry about. However, should you start typing the same tuple and are about to rewrite it, you will be notified by PyCharm about the existence of the same tuple stored before. Can you guess how? Go ahead and try writing the above example in PyCharm and see how you are notified.

PyCharm will highlight the name of the tuple for you, and that is an indication that you have already used the same name before. If this was the first occurrence, PyCharm will not highlight the name or the values for you at all.

Unpacking

Since we just discussed tuples, it is essential to know about a feature that has further simplified the use of tuples for us. Unpacking is quite useful. Suppose you have a few values stored in a tuple and you wish to assign each one of them to another variable individually. There are two ways you can do that; with or without the use of unpacking. Let us look at the first way of doing so and then we will look at the use of unpacking for comparison.

First method:

```
ages = (25, 30, 35, 40)
Drake = ages[0]
Emma = ages[1]
Sully = ages[2]
```

If you print these values now, you will see the ages accordingly. This means that the values stored within these individual variables were successfully taken from the tuple as we wanted. However, this was a little longer. What if we can do all of that in just one line?

Second method:

```
ages = (25, 30, 35, 40)
Drake, Emma, Sully, Sam = ages
```

Now, this looks much more interesting. Instead of using a number of lines, we got the same job done within the same line. Each individual variable still received the same age as the first method and each can be called upon to do exactly the same thing. This is how unpacking can work miracles for us. It saves you time and effort and allows us to maintain a clean, clear, and readable code for reference.

With that said, it is now time for us to be introduced to one of the most important elements within Python that is used both by beginners and experts almost every single time they program.

_ *Python Dictionaries*

Dictionaries are data structures that enable the memorization of the data in key-value couples.

```
AlumniAge = {'Andrea': 23,   'John': 28}
```

There are two keys—"Andrea" and "John." The value associated with key "Andrea" is "23," which is his age. The value associated with key "John" is "28," which is his age.

These are the simple things you should always remember while using a Python dictionary.

Keys in dictionaries are unique. Keys are immutable. You can always eliminate and add a new key, but you cannot update the key.

There are times you will come across certain information that is unique and holds a key value. Let us assume that you have to design software that can store information about customers or clients. This information may include names, numbers, emails, physical addresses, and so on. This is where dictionaries will come into play.

If you had thought that a dictionary in Python would be like your everyday dictionary for languages we speak, you might not have been completely wrong here. There is a similarity that we can see in these dictionaries. Every single entry that is made is unique. In Python, if an entry tries to replicate itself or if you try to store the same value again, you will be presented with an error.

So, how exactly do we use dictionaries? For that, let us switch back to our new best friend, PyCharm, and start typing a little.

Come up with an imaginary person's name, email address, age, and phone number. Don't start assigning these yet, as we would like to use the dictionary here for that. Ready? Okay, let us begin:

```
> user_one = {    #Dictionaries are represented by {}
>     'name': 'Sam',
>     'age': 40,
>     'phone': 123456789,
>     'married': False
> }
```

We have entered some information about a character named Sam. You can use the print command and run the dictionary named "user_one" and the system will print out these values for you.

For dictionaries, we use the colon (:) sign between values. The object name is placed in a string followed by the colon sign. After that, we use either a string, a number (integer or float), or a Boolean value. You can use these to assign every object with its unique key pair. In case you are confused, the key pair is just another way of saying the value that is assigned to the object. For example, the key pair for "name" is "Sam."

Now, let us try and see what happens if we add another "married" value. As soon as you are done typing, the system will highlight it. Note that you can still type in the new value and the system will continue to function. However, the value it will use will be the latest value it can find.

This means that if you initially set the value for married to False and later change it to True, it will only display True.

```
user_one = { #Dictionaries are represented by {}
'name': 'Sam',
'age': 40,
'phone': 123456789,
'married': False,
'married': True}
print(user_one['married'])
```

→ True

When it comes to calling values from the dictionary, we use the name of the string instead of the index number. If you try and run the index number zero, you will be presented with a 'KeyError: o' in the trace-back. Can you guess why that happens?

As stated previously, dictionaries store values that are unique. If you use a number or a name that does not exist within the defined dictionary, you will always end up with an error. You will need to know the exact name or value of the information you are trying to access.

Similarly, if you try to access "Phone" instead of "phone," you will get the same error as Python is case-sensitive and will not identify the former as an existing value.

Dictionaries can be updated easily should the situation call for it. Say we got the wrong phone number for our client stored as "user_one," we can simply use the following procedure to update the entry:

```
user_one['phone'] = 345678910
print(user_one['phone'])
```

You should now be able to see the new number we have stored. There's one little thing you may have noticed right about now when you did this. See the crazy wiggly lines which have appeared? These are here to suggest you rewrite the value instead of updating it separately to keep the code clean. PyCharm will continue to do this every now and then where it feels like you are causing the code to grow complicated. There is no reason for you to panic if you see these lines. However, if the lines are red, something is surely wrong and you may need to check on that.

Similarly, if you wish to add new key information to your dictionary, you can do so easily using almost the same process as shown here:

```
user_one['profession'] = 'programmer'
```

It is that easy! Try to print out the information now and you should be able to see this along with all previous entries available to you.

Lastly, you can use a method called "get" to stop the program from coming back with an error in case you or your program user enters a wrong or a missing value when calling upon a dictionary. You can also assign it a default value like a symbol to notify yourself or the user that this value does not exist or is not identifiable by the program itself. Here is a little example where the user has tried to find out information about "kids." We have provided it with a default value of "invalid":

```
print(user_one.get('kids', 'invalid'))
```

If you run this through, you will be presented with a result that shows an object named "invalid." We will make use of this feature in a more meaningful way in our test.

- clear(): Remove all items from the dictionary.
- copy(): Return a shallow copy of the dictionary.
- fromkeys(seq[, v]): Return a new dictionary with keys from seq and value equal to v (defaults to None).
- get(key[,d]): Return the value of key. If the key does not exist, return "d" (defaults to None).
- items(): Return a new view of the dictionary's items (key, value).
- keys(): Return a new view of the dictionary's keys.
- pop(key[,d]): Remove the item with a key and return its value or return "d" if the key is not found. If d is not provided and the key is not found, raises KeyError.
- popitem(): Remove and return an arbitrary item (key, value). Raises KeyError if the dictionary is empty.
- setdefault(key[,d]): If the key is in the dictionary, return its value. If not, insert key with a value of "d" and return d (defaults to None).
- update([other]): Update the dictionary with the key/value pairs from other, overwriting existing keys.
- values(): Return a new view of the dictionary's value

There are also some embedded functions that can be used with a dictionary:
- all(): Return True if all keys of the dictionary are true (or if the dictionary is empty).
- any(): Return True if any key of the dictionary is true. If the dictionary is empty, return False.
- len(): Return the length (the number of items) in the dictionary.
- cmp(): Compare items of two dictionaries.
- sorted(): Return a new sorted list of keys in the dictionary.

Chapter 10: Deep Dive on Python Tuples

_ *Tuple in Python*

A tuple is like a list, but we cannot edit its elements. This is one of the main differences that we will see with the tuple versus the list when we work in the Python language, and other coding languages as well.

For example, when we work with a list, we have different items that are available in the code, and we are able to change them, even when we execute the code. This is a benefit of the list; if you want to be able to change up some of the items and not have them set there for a long time, then you would want to work with the list.

On the other hand, the tuple is going to look similar in syntax to what we see with a list. But the elements are not changeable at all. If you want to work with an option that will keep the elements the same all of the time, once you are done putting them in place, then the tuple is going to be the best option for you.

Example:
Start IDLE.
Navigate to the File menu and click New Window.
Type the following:

```
tuple_mine = (21, 12, 31)
print(tuple_mine)
tuple_mine = (31, "Green", 4.7)
print(tuple_mine)
```

→ (21, 12, 31)
→ (31, 'Green', 4.7)

Accessing Python Tuple Elements

```
tuple_mine=('t','r','o','g','r','a','m')
print(tuple_mine[1])#output:'r'
print(tuple_mine[3])#output:'g'
```

_ *Negative Indexing*

Just like lists, tuples can also be indexed negatively.
Like lists, -1 refers to the last element on the list and -2 refer to the second last element.
Example:

Start IDLE.

Navigate to the File menu and click New Window.

Type the following:

```
tuple_mine=('t','r','o','g','r','a','m')
print(tuple_mine [-2])#the output will be 'a'
```

_ *Slicing*

The slicing operator, accessed by using the full colon (☺ is used to access a range of items in a tuple.

Example:

Start IDLE.

Navigate to the File menu and click New Window.

Type the following:

```
tuple_mine=('t','r','o','g','r','a','m')
print(tuple_mine [2:5])#Output: 'o','g','r'
print(tuple_mine[:-4])#Output: 't', 'r', 'o'
```

Important:

Tuple elements are immutable meaning they cannot be changed. However, we can combine elements in a tuple using +(concatenation operator). We can also repeat elements in a tuple using the * operator, just like lists.

Example:

Start IDLE.

Navigate to the File menu and click New Window.

Type the following:

```
print((7, 45, 13) + (17, 25, 76))
print(("Several",) * 4)
```

→ (7, 45, 13, 17, 25, 76)

→ ('Several', 'Several', 'Several', 'Several')

Since we cannot change elements in a tuple, we cannot delete the elements either. However, removing the full tuple can be attained using the keyword del.

Example:

Start IDLE.

Navigate to the File menu and click New Window.

Type the following:

```
t_mine=['t','k','q','v','y','c','d']
del t_mine
```

_Inbuilt Python Functions with Tuple

Method	Description	Method	Description
enumerate()	Return an enumerate object. It contains the index and value of all the items of a tuple as pairs.	Tuple()	Convert an iterable to a tuple.
Sorted()	Take elements in the tuple and return a new sorted list. It does not sort the tuple itself.	Max()	Return the largest element in the tuple.
All()	Return True if all elements of the tuple are true, or if the tuple is empty.	Sum()	Return the sum of all elements in the tuple.
Len()	Return the length (the number of items) in the tuple.	Min()	Return the smallest item in the tuple.
		Any()	Return True if any element of the tuple is true. If the tuple is empty, return False.

_Escape Sequences in Python

The escape sequences enable us to format our output to enhance clarity to the human user. A program will still run successfully without using escape sequences, but the output will be highly confusing to the human user. Writing and displaying output in expected output is part of good programming practices. The following are commonly used escape sequences:

Method	Description	Method	Description
\n	ASCII Linefeed	\b	ASCII Backspace
\"	Double quote	\\	Backslash
\f	ASCII Formfeed	\a	ASCII Bell
\newline	Backslash and newline ignored	\'	Single quote
\r	ASCII Carriage Return	\t	ASCII Horizontal Tab

\v	ASCII Vertical Tab	\ooo	Character with oc-tal value ooo
\xHH	The character with hexadecimal value HH		

Example:

Start your IDLE.

Navigate to the File menu and click New Window.

Type the following:

```
print("D:\\Lessons\\Programming")
print("Prints\n in two lines")
```

→ D:\Lessons\Programming

→ Prints

→ in two lines

Integers, floating-point, and complex numbers are supported in Python and all help convert different number data types. The presence or absence of a decimal point separates integers and floating points. For instance, 4 is an integer while 4.0 is a floating-point number. Programmers often need to convert decimal numbers into octal, hexadecimal, or binary forms. We can represent binary, hexadecimal, and octal systems in Python by simply placing a prefix to the particular number. Sometimes referred to as coercion, type conversion allows us to change one type of number into another.

Inbuilt functions such as int() allow us to convert data types directly. The same functions can be used to convert from strings. We create a list in Python by placing items called elements inside square brackets separated by commas. In programming and Python specifically, the first time is always indexed zero. For a list of five items, we will access them from index 0 to index 4. Failure to access the items in a list in this manner will create an index error.

Chapter 11: Sets in Python

_ *Sets*

A Python set is an unordered collection containing unique items. While sets are mutable, meaning we can add and remove items to and from them, each item in a set must be immutable. One important thing about sets is that you cannot have any duplicate items in them. We usually use sets to do mathematical operations, such as union, intersection, complement, and difference.

Unlike a sequence type, a set type doesn't provide any slicing or indexing operations. The values do not have any keys associated with them like dictionaries do. Python contains two types of sets—mutable sets and immutable frozensets. Each type of set is created with a set of curly braces containing values separated by a comma. An empty set cannot be created using the curly braces, as a={} will create a dictionary! Empty sets are created by using a=set() or a=frozenset().

Below are the methods and the operations for sets:

len(s) → will return how many elements are in (s).

s.copy() → will return a shallow copy of (s).

s.difference(t) → will return a set containing the items in (s) but not (t).

s.intersection(t) → will return a set containing the items in both (s) and (t).

s.isdisjoint(t) → will return True if there are no common items between (s) and (t).

s.issubset(t) → will return True if the contents of (s) are in (t).

s.issuperset(t) → will return True if the contents of (t) are in (s).

s.symmetric_difference(t) → will return a set of the items from (s) or (t) but not those in both.

s.union(t) → will return a set containing the items in (s) or (t).

The parameter of (t) may be any object in Python that will support iteration with any method that is available to the objects set and frozenset. Be aware, if you need to use an operator version of these methods, you must set the arguments—the methods themselves will accept any type that is iterable. Below are the operator versions of the methods:

Operator Methods

Make two sets:

```
s = {"cake", "apple", "banana"}
t = {"humans", "cake", "86etroit"}
```

The following will return the difference between s and t:

```
print(s.difference(t))
```
→ {'banana', 'apple'}

The following will return True if "s" is a subset of "t" and False if "s" is not a subset of "t":

```
print(s.issubset(t))
```
→ False

The following will return True if "s" is a superset of "t" and False if "s" is not a superset of "t":

```
s.issuperset(t)
```
→ False

The following will return the "s" set with all the items of "s" and "t" excluding the common items:

```
s.symmetric_difference(t)
```
→ {'apple', 'detroit', 'humans', 'banana'}

The following will return a new set with elements from the set passed through argument and the original set in a randomized order. If the argument is left empty, then it will return the same set in randomized order.

```
s.union(t)
```
→ {'apple', 'humans', 'cake', 'detroit', 'banana'}

```
s.union()
```
→ {'banana', 'apple', 'cake'}

For the mutable set objects, there are some extra methods:

s.add(item) → will add the item to (s). If the item is already there, nothing will happen.

s.clear() → will remove all items from (s).

s.difference_update(t) → will remove items in (s) that are also in (t).

s.discard(item) → will remove the specified item from (s).

s.intersection_update(t) → will remove items from (s) that do not appear in the intersection of (s) and (t).

s.pop() → will return and remove a given arbitrary item from (s).

s.remove(item) → will remove the specified item from (s).

s.symmetric_difference_update(t) → will remove items from (s) that cannot be found in the symmetric difference of (s) and (t).

s.update(t) → will add the items from iterable (t) to (s).

The next example will show you a few set operations and the results:

```
s1={'ab', 3, 4, (5, 6)}
s2={'ab', 7, (7, 6)}
print(s1-s2) # identical to s1.difference (s2)
```
Running this code will return:

→ {(5, 6), 3, 4}

```
print(s1.intersection(s2))
```

Running this code will return:

→ {'ab'}

```
print(s1.union(s2))
```

Running this code will return:

→ { 'ab', 3, 4, 7, (5, 6), (7, 6)}

The set object is not bothered if its members are of different types; they just have to all be immutable. If you were to try using mutable objects in your set, like a list or a dictionary, an unhashable type error will be thrown. All hashable types have a hash value that remains the same through the entire lifecycle of the instance and all of the built-in immutable types are of a hashable type. The built-in mutable types are not of a hashable type, so they cannot be included in sets as elements or as dictionary keys.

Note, when the s1 and the s2 union is printed, there is just one "ab'" value. Remember, sets do not include any duplicates. As well as the built-in methods, there are several other operations that can be performed on a set. For example, if you wanted to test a set for membership, you would do the following:

```
print('ab' in s1)
```

Running this code will return:

→ True

```
print('ab' not in s1)
```

Running this code will return:

→ False

Looping through the elements of a set would look like this:

```
for element in s1:
    print(element)
```

→ (5, 6)
→ ab
→ 3
→ 4

Immutable Sets

As mentioned earlier, Python has an immutable set type known as frozenset. It works much the same as set does but with one difference: You cannot use any operation or method that can change values, such as the clear() or add() methods. Immutability can be quite useful in a number of ways. For example, a normal set is mutable, which means it is not hashable and that, in turn, means that it cannot be a member of another set. On the other hand, a frozenset can be a member of another set because it is immutable. Plus, this immutability of frozenset means that it can be used as a dictionary key, like this:

```
fs1 = frozenset(s1)
fs2 = frozenset(s2)
print({fs1: 'fs1', fs2: 'fs2'})
```

Running this code will return:

→ { frozenset({(5, 6), 3, 4, 'ab'}): 'fs1', frozenset({(7, 6), 'ab', 7}); 'fs2'}

_ *Modules for Algorithms and Data Structures*

In addition to these built-in types, Python has a few modules that can be used for extending those built-in functions and types. Much of the time, the modules may be more efficient and may offer advantages in programming terms that let us make our code simpler.

Up to now, we have examined the built-in types for dictionaries, lists, sets, and strings. These are often termed as abstract data types (ADTs) and may be considered to be mathematical specifications for the operations that may be performed on the data. Their behavior is what defines them, not their implementation. Aside from the ADTs we already looked at, there are a few Python libraries that include extensions for the built-in datatypes; we'll be looking at these next.

Collections

The module called collections contains alternatives for these data types—high-performance, specialized alternatives—in addition to a utility function for the creation of named tuples. Below are the datatypes, the operations, and what they do:

namedtuple() → will create a tuple subclass with the given fields.

Deque → will provide lists that have fast appends and that pop at either end.

ChainMap → a class much like a dictionary that will create a single view showing multiple mappings.

Counter → a dictionary subclass that will count hashable objects.

OrderedDict → a dictionary subclass that will remember the order of entries.

Defaultdict → a dictionary subclass that will call a function that can supply the missing values:
- UserDict
- UserList
- UserString

These datatypes are used as wrappers for the base class that underlies each one. We don't tend to use these very much now but rather subclass the base classes. They can, however, be used for accessing the underlying objects as attributes.

Deques

A deque (pronounced deck) is a double-ended queue. These objects are similar to lists with support for appends that are thread-safe and memory-efficient. A deque is mutable and has support for some of the list operations, like indexing. You can assign a deque by index, but you cannot slice one directly. For example, if you tried dq[1:2], you would get a Type Error; there is a way to do it, though, and we'll look at that later. The biggest advantage of using a deque instead of a list is that it is much faster to insert an item at the start of a deque than it is at the start of a list. That said, it isn't always faster to insert items at the end of a deque. All deques are thread-safe and we can serialize them using a module called pickle.

Perhaps one of the most useful ways to use a deque is for the population and consummation of items, since these actions happen sequentially from each end.

```
from collections import deque
dq = deque('abc') #the deque is created
dq.append('d') #value 'd' is added on the right
dq.appendleft('z') # value 'z' is added on the left
dq.extend('efg') # multiple items are added on the right
dq.extendleft('yxw') # multiple items are added on the left
print(dq)
```

Running this code will return:

→ deque(['w', 'x', 'y', 'z', 'a', 'b', 'c', 'd', 'e', 'f', 'g'])

To consume items in our deque, we can use the pop() and popleft() methods:

```
print(dq.pop()) #item on the right is returned and removed
```

Running this code will return:

→ 'g'

```
print(dq.popleft()) # item on the left is returned and removed
```

Running this code will return:

→ 'w'

```
print(dq)
```

Running this code will return:

→ deque(['x', 'y', 'z', 'a', 'b', 'c', 'd', 'e', 'f'])

We also have a method called rotate(n) which moves and rotates any item of n steps right for positive n integer values and left for negative n integer values, with positive integers used for the argument:

```
dq.rotate(2) #all the items are moved 2 steps to the right
print(dq)
```

Running this code will return:

→ deque(['e', 'f', 'x', 'y', 'z', 'a', 'b', 'c', 'd'])

```
dq.rotate(-2) # all the items are moved 2 steps to the left
print(dq)
```

Running this code will return:

→ deque(['x', 'y', 'z', 'a', 'b', 'c', 'd', 'e', 'f'])

We can also use these pop() and rotate() methods to delete elements. The way to return a slice as a list is as follows:

```
print(dq)
```

Running this code will return:

→ deque(['x', 'y', 'z', 'a', 'b', 'c', 'd', 'e', 'f'])

```
import itertools
print(list(itertools.islice(dq, 3, 9)))
```

Running this code will return:

→ ['a', 'b', 'c', 'd', 'e', 'f']

The iertools.islice() method is the same as a slice on a list, but instead of the argument being a list, it is an iterable and selected values are returned as a list, using start and stop indices.

One of the more useful deque features is that a maxlen parameter is supported as optional and used for restricting the deque size. This is ideal for circular buffers, a type of data structure that is fixed in size and is connected end to end. These tend to be used when data streams are to be buffered. Here is an example:

```
dq2=deque([],maxlen=3)
for I in range(6):
    dq2.append(i)
    print(dq2)
```

We have populated from the right and consumed from the left. As soon as the buffer has been filled, the older values are consumed, and new values come in from the right.

Chapter 12: Functions in Python

Creating and calling a function is easy. The primary purpose of a function is to allow you to organize, simplify, and modularize your code. Whenever you have a set of code that you will need to execute in sequence from time to time, defining a function for that set of code will save you time and space in your program. Instead of repeatedly typing code or even copy-pasting, you simply define a function.

We began with almost no prior knowledge about Python except for a clue that it was some kind of programming language that is in great demand these days. Now, look at you; creating simple programs, executing codes, and fixing small-scale problems on your own. Not bad at all! However, learning always comes to a point where things can get rather trickier.

In quite a similar fashion, functions are docile-looking things; you call them when you need to get something done. But did you know that these functions have so much going on at the back? Imagine every function as a mini-program. It is also written by programmers like us to carry out specific things without us having to write lines and lines of code. You only do it once, save it as a function, and then call the function where it is applicable or needed.

The time has come for us to dive into a complex world of functions where we not only learn how to use them effectively, but also look into what goes on behind these functions and how we can come up with our own personalized function. This will be slightly challenging, but I promise there are more references that you will enjoy to keep the momentum going.

How to Define and Call a Function

To start, we need to take a look at how we are able to define our own functions in this language. The function in Python is going to be defined when we use the statement of "def" and follow it with a function name and some parentheses. This lets the compiler know that you are defining a function, and which function you would like to define at this time as well. There are going to be a few rules in place when it comes to defining one of these functions though, and it is important to do these in the proper manner to ensure your code acts in the way you would like. Some of the Python rules that we need to follow for defining these functions will include the following:

1. Any of the arguments or input parameters that you would like to use have to be placed within the parentheses so the compiler knows what is going on.

2. The function first statement can be an optional statement; something like a documentation string that goes with your function if needed.

3. The code that is found within all of the functions that we are working with needs to start out with a colon and be indented.

4. The statement return that we get, or the expression, will need to exit a function at this time. We can then have the option of passing back a value to the caller. A return statement that doesn't have an argument with it is going to give us the same return as none.

Before we get too familiar with some of the work that can be done with these Python functions, we need to take some time to understand the rules of indentation when we are declaring these functions in Python.

The same kinds of rules are going to be applicable to some of the other elements of Python as well, such as declaring conditions, variables, and loops, so learning how this work can be important here.

You will find that Python is going to follow a particular style when it comes to indentation to help define the code because the functions in order languages are not going to have any explicit begin or end, like curly braces, to help indicate the start and the stop for that function. This is why we are going to rely on indentation. When we work with the proper kind of indentation here, we are able to really see some good results and ensure that the compiler is going to know when a function is being used.

_ *Understanding Functions Better*

Functions are like containers that store lines of codes within themselves, just like variables that contain one specific value. There are two types of functions we get to deal with in Python. The first are built-in or pre-defined, and the others are custom-made or user-created.

Either way, each function has a specific task that it can carry out. The code that is written before creating any function is what gives that function identity and a task. Now, the function knows what it needs to do whenever it is called in.

When we began our journey, we wrote "I made it!" on the console as our first program. We used our first function there as well: the print() function. Functions are generally identified by parentheses that follow the name of the function. Within these parentheses, we pass arguments called parameters. Some functions accept a certain kind of parenthesis while others accept different ones.

Let us look a little deeper and see how functions greatly help us reduce our work and better organize our codes. Imagine, we have a program that runs during the live streaming of an event. The purpose of the program is to provide our users with a customized greeting. Imagine just how many times you would need to write the same code again and again if there were quite a few users who decide to join your stream. With functions, you can cut down on your own work easily.

In order for us to create a function, we first need to 'define' the same. That is where a keyword called 'def' comes along. When you start typing 'def' Python immediately knows you are about to define a function. You will see the color of the three letters change to orange (if using PyCharm as your IDE). That is another sign of confirmation that Python knows what you are about to do.

```
def say_hi():
```

Here, say_hi is the name I have decided to go with, though you can choose any that you prefer. Remember, keep your name descriptive so that it is understandable and easy to read for anyone. After you have named your function, follow it up with parentheses. Lastly, add the friendly old colon to let Python know we are about to add a block of code. Press enter to start a new indented line.

Now, we shall print out two statements for every user who will join the stream.

```
print""Hello there"")
print''Welcome to My Live Stream'')
```

After this, give two lines of space to take away those wiggly lines that appear the minute you start typing something else. Now, to have this printed out easily, just call the function by typing its name and run the program. In our case, it would be:

```
say_hi()
```

→ Hello there!
→ Welcome to My Live Stream!

See how easily this can work for us in the future? We do not have to repeat this over and over again. Let's make this function a little more interesting by giving it a parameter. Right at the top line, where it says "def say_hi()"? Let us add a parameter here. Type in the word 'name' as a parameter within the parenthesis. The word should be greyed out to confirm that Python has understood it as a parameter.

Now, you can use this to your advantage and further personalize the greetings to something like this:

If you are doing it on shell, you need to delete the previously defined function with:

```
del say_hi
```

Now let's write the new function:

```
def say_hi(user):
    print(""Hello there, {user}"")
    print''Welcome to My Live Stream'')


user = input""Please enter your name to begin:"")
say_hi(user)
```

The output would now ask the user regarding their name. This will then be stored into a variable called user. Since this is a string value, say_hi() should be able to accept this easily. By passing "user" as an argument, we get this as an output:

→ Please enter your name to begin: Johnny
→ Hello there, Johnny!
→ Welcome to My Live Stream!

Now that's more like it! Personalized to perfection. We can add as many lines as we want; the function will continue to update itself and provide greetings to various users with different names.

There may be times where you may need more than just the user's first name. You might want to inquire about the last name of the user as well. To add to that, add this to the first line and follow the same accordingly:

```
def say_hi(first_name, last_name):
    print(""Hello there, {first_name} {last_name}"")
    print''Welcome to My Live Stream'')

first_name = input""Enter your first name:"")
last_name = input""Enter your last name:"")
say_hi(first_name, last_name)
```

Now, the program will begin by asking the user for their first name, followed by the last name. Once that is sorted, the program will provide a personalized greeting with both the first and last names.

However, these are positional arguments, meaning that each value you input is in order. If you were to change the positions of the names for John Doe, Doe will become the first name and John will become the last name. You may wish to remain a little careful on that.

Hopefully, now you have a good idea of what functions are and how you can access and create them. Now, we will jump towards the more complex front of return statements.

"Wait! There's more?" Well, I could have explained. However, you may not have understood it completely. Since we have covered all the bases, it is appropriate enough for us to see exactly what these are and how these get along with functions.

_ *Return Statement*

Return statements are useful when you wish to create a function whose sole job is to return some values. These could be for users or for programmers alike. It is a lot easier if we do this instead of talk about theories, so let's jump back to our PyCharm and create another function.

Let us start by defining a function called cube which will basically multiply a number by itself three times. However, since we want Python to return a value, we will use the following code:

```
def cube(number):
    return number * number * number
```

By typing "return," you are informing Python that you wish for it to return a value to you that can later be stored in a variable or used elsewhere. It is pretty much like the input() function where a user enters something and it gets returned to us.

```
def cube(number):
    return number * number * number

number = int(input""Enter the number:""))
print(cube(number))
```

Go ahead and try out the code to see how it works. It is not necessary that we define functions such as these. You can create your own complex functions that convert kilos into pounds, miles into kilometers, or even carry out far greater and more complex jobs. The only limit is your imagination. The more you practice, the more you explore.

With that said, it is time to say goodbye to the world of functions and head into the advanced territories of Python. By now, you already have all you need to know to start writing your own codes.

_ Multiple Parameters

You can assign two or more parameters in a function. For exampl e:

```
def simpOp(x, y):
    z = x + y
    return z

print(simpOp(1, 2))
```
　→ 3

_ Lambda Function

Anonymous Functions or Lambda

Using an anonymous function is a convenient way to write one-line functions that require arguments and return a value. It uses the keyword lambda. Despite having the purpose of being a one liner, it can have numerous parameters. For exampl e:

```
average = lambda x, y, z: (x + y + z) / 3
x = average(10, 20, 30)
print(x)
```
　→ 20.0

```
print(average(12, 51, 231))
```
→ 98.0

Global Variables

Global variables are multipurpose variables used in any part of the Python environment. The variable used can operate in your program or module while in any part.

Local Variables

Unlike global variables, local variables are used locally, declared within a Python function or module, and utilized solely in a specific program or Python module. When implemented outside particular modules or tasks, the Python interpreter will fail to recognize the units henceforth throwing an error message for un-declared values.

Python has two built-in methods named globals() and locals(). They allow you to determine whether a variable is either part of the global namespace or the local namespace. The following example shows how to use these methods:

```
def calc():
    global place
    place =""Rom""
    name =""Le""

    print""place in global"",''plac'' in globals())
    print""place in local "",''plac'' in locals())
    print""name in global "",''nam'' in globals())
    print""name in local  "",''nam'' in locals())
    return

place =""Berli""
print(place)
calc()
```

Chapter 13: Modules in Python

What are the Modules?

In Python, a module is a portion of a program (an extension file) that can be invoked through other programs without having to write them in every program used. Besides, they can define classes and variables. These modules contain related sentences between them and can be used at any time. The use of the modules is based on using a code (program body, functions, variables) already stored on it called import. With the use of the modules, it can be observed that Python allows for simplifying programs a lot because it allows us to simplify problems into smaller ones to make the code shorter. This way, programmers do not get lost when looking for something in hundreds of coding lines when making codes.

How to Create a Module

To create a module in Python, we do"t need a lot.

For example: if you want to create a module that prints a city, we write our code in the editor and save it as""mycity.py""

Once this is done, we will know that this will be the name of our module (omitting the .py sentence), which will be assigned to the global variable __city__.

But, beyond that, we can see that the file""mycity.p"" is not complicated at all, since the only thing inside is a function called""print_cit"" which will have a string as a parameter and will print""Hello, welcome to"" This will concatenate with the string that was entered as a parameter.

Locate a Module

When importing a module, the interpreter automatically searches the same module for its current address, if this is not available, Python (or its interpreter) will perform a search on the PYTHONPATH environment variable that is nothing more than a list containing directory names with the same syntax as the environment variable.

If in any particular case these previous actions failed, Python would look for a default UNIX path (located in /user/local/lib/python on Windows).

The modules are searched in the directory list given by the variable sys.path.

This variable contains the current directory, the PYTHONPATH directory, and the entire directory that comes by default in the installation.

_ *Import Statement*

This statement is used to import a module. Through any Python code file, its process is as follows: The Python interpreter searches the file system for the current directory where it is executed. Then, the interpreter searches for its predefined paths in its configuration.

When it meets the first match (the name of the module), the interpreter automatically executes it from start to finish. When importing a module for the first time, Python will generate a compiled .pyc extension file. This extension file will be used in the following imports of this module. When the interpreter detects that the module has already been modified since the last time it was generated, it will generate a new module.

You must save the imported file in the same directory where Python is using the import statement so that Python can find it.

As we could see in our example, importing a module allows us to improve the functionalities of our program through external files.

Now, le"s see some examples. The first one is a calculator where will create a module that performs all the mathematical functions and another program that runs the calculator itself.

The first thing we do is the module""calculator.p"" which is responsible for doing all the necessary operations. Among them are addition, subtraction, division, and multiplication, as you can see.

We included the use of conditional statements such as if, else, and elif. We also included the use of exceptions so that the program will not get stuck every time the user enters an erroneous value at the numbers of the calculator for the division.

After that, we will create a program that will have to import the module previously referred to so that it manages to do all the pertinent mathematical functions.

But at this time, you might be thinking that the only existing modules are the ones that the programmer creates. This would be untrue, since Python has modules that come integrated into it.

With them, we will make two more programs: The first one is an improvement of the one that we have just done, and the second one will be an alarm that will print a string onscreen periodically.

Example
Create a Python module called dummymodule.py and write the following inside:

```
def testF():
    print""this is a module, goodbye"")
```

save the module as dummymodule.py in the Python installation directory.

In the shell:

```
import dummymodule
```

Now call the function:

```
dummymodule.testF()
```

You have used your first module.

_ *Module Example One*

The first thing that was done was to create the module, but at first sight, we have a surprise, which is that math was imported.

What does that mean to us?
Well, this means that we are acquiring the properties of the math module that comes by default in Python.

We see that the calculator function is created that has several options.
If the op value is equal to 1, the addition operation is made.
If it is equal to 2, the subtraction operation is made, and so on.

If op is equal to 5, it will return the value of the square root of the values num1 and num2 through the use of math.sqrt(num1), which returns the result of the root.

Then, if op is equal to 6, using functions "math.radians()" which means that num1 or num2 will become radians since that is the type of value accepted by the functions "math.sin()," meaning the value of the sine of num1 and num2 will return to us, which will be numbers entered by users arbitrarily who will become radians and then the value of the corresponding sine.

The last thing will be to create the main program, as it can be seen next:
Here, we can see the simple program, since it only imports the module "calculator.py," then the variables num1 and num2 are assigned the value by using an input.
Finally, an operation is chosen and, to finish, the calculator function of the calculator module is called, to which we will pass three parameters.

Module Example Two

We are going to create a module, which has within itself a function that acts as a chronometer in such a way that it returns true in case time ends.

In this module, as you can see, another module is imported called "time." It functions to operate with times and has a wide range of functions, from returning dates and times to helping create chronometers, for example.

The first thing we do is create the cron() function, which starts declaring that the start Alarm variables will be equal to time.time. With this, we are giving an initial value to this function equal to the exact moment the function enters an infinite cycle.

Since the restriction is always True, this cycle will never end unless the break command is inside of it.

Next, within the while cycle, there are several instructions.

The first is that the final variable is equal to time.time() to take into account the specific moment we are at to monitor time.

After that, another variable is created called times, and this acquires the value of the final minus start Alarm. But you will be wondering what the round function does. It rounds up values, which helps the program run easier. But this is not enough, so we use an "if since": If the subtraction between the end and the beginning is greater or equal to 60, then one minute was completed.

Why 60?

The time module works in seconds and for a minute to elapse, 60 seconds have to have elapsed. Therefore, the difference between the end and the beginning has to be greater than or equal to 60. In the affirmative case, True will be returned and we will get out of the infinite cycle.

Once the alarm module is finished, we proceed to make the program, and imports two modules, alarm (the one we created) and time.

The first thing we do is create the variable s as an input which asks the user if they want to start.

If the answer is affirmative, then the variable h representing the time will be equal to "time.strftime ("%H:%M:%S")," which means that we are using a function of the time module that returns the hour in the specified format so that it can then be printed using the print function.

The next action is to use the alarm module using the command alarm.cron(), which means that the cron() function is being called.

When this function is finished, the time will be assigned to the variable h, again, to finish printing it and be able to observe its correct operation.

As a conclusion of this chapter, we can say that the modules are fundamental for the proper performance of the programmer since they allow for more legible code as well as subdividing the problems to attack them from one to one and thus carrying out tasks easily.

Chapter 14: Files Handling in Python

The next thing that we need to focus on when it comes to working with Python is making sure we know how to handle files. It may happen that you are working with some data and you want to store them while ensuring that they are accessible for you to pull up and use when they are needed later. You do have some choices in the way you save the data, how they are going to be found later on, and how they are going to react in your code.

When working with files, you will find that there are a few operations or methods that you are able to choose from, including:

- Closing up a file you are working on,
- Creating a brand new file to work on, or
- Seeking out or moving a file over to a new location to make it easier to find.

Creating New Files

The first task that we are going to look at doing is creating a file. It is hard to do the other tasks if we don't first have a file in place to help us out. If you would like to be able to make a new file, you first need to make sure the file is opened up inside of your IDLE. Then, you can choose the mode that you would like to use when you write out your code.

When it comes to creating files on Python, you will find there are three modes that you are able to work with. The three main modes that we are going to focus on here are append (a), mode (x), and write (w).

Any time that you would like to open up a file and make some changes to it, you want to use the write mode. This is the easiest of the three to work with. The write method is going to make it easier for you to get the right parts of the code set up and working for you in the end.

The write function will ensure that you can make any additions and changes that you would like to the file. You can add new information to the file, change what is there, and so much more. If you would like to see what you can do with this part of the code with the write method, then you will want to open up your compiler and write the following code:

```
#file handling operations
#writing to a new file hello.txt
f = open('hello.txt', 'w', encoding = 'utf-8')
f.write("Hello Python Developers!")
f.write("Welcome to Python World")
f.flush()
f.close()
```

From here, we need to assess what you can do with the directories that we are working with. The default directory is always going to be the current directory. You are able to go through and switch up the directory where the code information is stored, but you have to take the time, in the beginning, to change that information up, or it isn't going to end up in the directory that you would like.

Whatever directory you spent your time when working on the code is the one you need to make your way back to when you want to find the file later on. If you would like it to show up in a different directory, make sure that you move over to that one before you save it and the code. With the option that we wrote above, when you go to the current directory (or the directory that you chose for this endeavor), you will be able to open up the file and see the message that you wrote out there.

For this one, we wrote a simple part of the code. You, of course, will be writing out codes that are much more complicated as we go along. And with those codes, there are going to be times when you would like to edit or overwrite some of what is in that file. This is possible to do with Python, and it just needs a small change to the syntax that you are writing out. A good example of what you can do with this one includes:

```
#file handling operations
#writing to a new file hello.txt
f = open('hello.txt', 'w', encoding = 'utf-8')
f.write("Hello Python Developers!")
f.write("Welcome to Python World")
mylist = ["Apple", "Orange", "Banana"]
#writelines() is used to write multiple lines into the file
f.write(str(mylist))
f.flush()
f.close()
```

The example above is a good one to use when you want to make a few changes to a file that you worked on before because you just need to add in one new line. This example wouldn't need to use that third line because it just has some simple words, but you can add in anything that you want to the program, just use the syntax above and change it up for what you need.

What Are Binary Files?

One other thing that we need to focus on for a moment before moving on is the idea of writing out some of your files and your data in the code as a binary file. This may sound a bit confusing, but it is a simple thing that Python will allow you to do. All that you need to do is take your data and change it over to a sound or image file, rather than having it as a text file.

With Python, you can change any of the code that you want into a binary file. It doesn't matter what kind of file it was in the past. But you do need to make sure that you work on the data in the right way to ensure that it is easier to expose in the way that you want later on. The syntax that is going to be needed to ensure that this will work well for you will be below:

```
# write binary data to a file
# writing the file hello.dat write binary mode
f = open('hello.dat', 'wb')
# writing as byte strings
f.write("I am writing data in binary file! ".encode(encoding='UTF-8'))
f.write("Let's write another list".encode(encoding='UTF-8'))
f.close()
```

If you take the time to use this code in your files, it is going to help you to make the binary file that you would like. Some programmers find that they like using this method because it helps them to get things in order and will make it easier to pull the information up when you need it.

_ Opening Your File

So far, we have worked with writing and saving a new file as well as working with a binary file. In these examples, we got some of the basics of working with files down so that you can make them work for you and you can pull them up any time that you would like.

Now that this part is done, it is time to learn how to open up the file and use it, and later even make changes to it, any time that you would like. Once you open that file up, it is going to be so much easier to use it again and again as much as you would like. When you are ready to see the steps that are needed to open up a file and use it, you will need the following syntax:

```
# read binary data to a file
# writing the file hello.dat write append binary mode
with open("hello.dat", 'rb') as f:
    data = f.read()
text = data.decode('utf-8')
print(text)
```

The output that you would get from putting this into the system would be like the following:

→ I am writing data in binary file! Let's write another list

Finally, we need to take a look at how you can seek out some of the files that you need in this kind of coding language.

For example, say you are working on a file and find that things are not showing up the way that you would like for them to. Maybe you didn't spell the time of the identifier the right way, or the directory is not where you want it to be. The seek option may be the best way to actually find this lost file and make the changes so it is easier to find later on.

With this method, you are going to be able to change where you place the file to ensure that it is going to be in the right spot all of the time or even to make it a bit easier for you to find it when you need. You just need to use syntax like what is above to help you make these changes.

Working through all of the different methods that we have talked about here is going to help you to do a lot of different things inside of your code. Whether you would like to make a new file, change up the code, move the file around, or more; you will be able to do it all using the codes that we have gone through here.

Chapter 15: Exception Handling in Python

The next topic that we need to spend some time exploring in this guidebook is the idea of exception handling. There are going to be times when your code presents some errors or other problems inside the code that you are working on, and this is where the exception is going to occur. Knowing when to recognize these exceptions, how to handle them, and even how to make some of your own can make a big difference in how well you are able to do some of your own coding in Python.

A good example of an exception that your compiler is automatically going to raise is when you or the user is to divide by zero. The compiler is then going to recognize that this is something the user is not able to do, and it is going to send out that exception as an alert. It can also be something that is going to be called up if you, as the programmer, are trying to call up a function and the name is not spelled in the proper manner so there is no match present to bring up.

There are a few different exceptions that are automatically found in your Python library. It is a good idea to take some time to look through them and recognize these exceptions so you can recognize them later on. Some of the most common exceptions that you need to worry about are as follows:

- Finally—this is the action that you will want to use to perform cleanup actions, whether the exceptions occur or not.
- Assert—this condition is going to trigger the exception inside of the code.
- Raise—the raise command is going to trigger an exception manually inside of the code.
- Try/except—this is when you want to try out a block of code and then it is recovered thanks to the exceptions that either you or the Python code rose.

Raising an Exception

Now that we know a bit more about these exceptions and what they mean, we need to look at how to write one out and some of the steps that you can use if one of these does end up in your own code. If you are going through some of the code writing, and you start to notice that an exception will be raised, know that often the solution is going to be a simple one. But, as the programmer, you need to take the time to get this fixed. To help us get started here, let's take a look at what the syntax of the code for raising an exception is all about:

```
x = 10
y = 0
result = x/y #trying to divide by zero
print(result)
```

The output that you are going to get when you try to get the interpreter to go through this code would be:

→ Traceback (most recent call last):
→ File "D: \Python34\tt.py", line 3, in <module>
→ result = x/y
→ ZeroDivisionError: division by zero

As we take a moment to look at the example that we have here, we can see that the program is going to bring up an exception for us, mainly because we are trying to divide a number by zero and this is something that is not allowed in Python code (and any other coding language for that matter). If you decide not to make any changes at this point and you go ahead and run the program as it is, you could end up with the compiler sending you an error message. The code is going to tell the user the problem, but as you can see, the problem is not listed out in an easy-to-understand method and it is likely the user will have no idea what is going on or how they can fix the problem at all.

With that example that we worked on above, you have some options. You can choose to leave the message that is kind of confusing if you don't know any coding, or you can add in a new message that is easier to read and explains why this error has been raised in the first place. It won't have a lot of numbers and random letters that only make sense to someone who has done coding for a bit, which makes the whole thing a bit more user-friendly overall. The syntax that you can use to control the message that your user is going to see is:

```python
x = 10
y = 0
try:
    result = x/y
    print(result)
except ZeroDivisionError:
    print("You are trying to divide by zero.")
```

Take a look at the two codes above. The one that we just did looks a little bit similar to the one above it, but this one has a message inside. This message is going to show up when the user raises this particular exception. You won't get the string of letters and numbers that don't make sense, and with this one, the user will know exactly what has gone wrong and can fix that error.

Can I Define My Own Exceptions?

In the examples above, we took some time to define and handle the exceptions that the compiler offered to us and are already found in the Python library. Now it is time for us to take it a bit further and learn how to raise a few of our own exceptions in any kind of code that we want to write. Maybe you are working on a code that only allows for a few choices to the user, one that only allows them to pick certain numbers, or one that only allows them to have so many chances at guessing. These are common things that we see when we work with gaming programs but can work well in other programs that you design.

When you make these kinds of exceptions, the compiler is going to have to be told that an exception is being raised, because it is not going to see that there is anything wrong in this part of the code. The programmer has to go in and let the compiler know what rules it has to follow, and what exceptions need to be raised in the process. A good example of the syntax that you can use to make this happen in your own code will be below:

```
class CustomException(Exception):
    def _init_(self, value):
        self.parameter = value
    def _str_(self):
        return repr(self.parameter)

try:
    CustomException("This is a CustomError!")
except CustomException as ex:
    print("Caught:", ex.parameter)
```

In this code, you have been successful in setting up your own exceptions and whenever the user raises one of these exceptions, the message of "Caught: This is a CustomError!" is going to come up on the screen. This is the best way to show your users that you have added a customer exception into the program, especially if this is just one that you personally created for this part of the code, and not one that the compiler is going to recognize on its own.

Just like with the other examples that we went through, we worked with some generic wording just to show how exceptions are able to work. You can easily go through and change this up so that you get a message that is unique for the code that you are writing and will explain to the user what is going on if they get the error message.

Learning how to work with some of the exceptions that can come up in your code is one of the best ways to make sure that your codes work the way that you want, that the user is going to like working with your program, and that everything is going to proceed as normal and do what you want. Take some time to practice these examples and see how they can work for you in order to handle any of the exceptions that come up in your code.

Chapter 16: Objects and Classes in Python

We have already mentioned that Python is an object-oriented programming language. There are other languages that are procedure-oriented that emphasize functions, but in Python, the stress is on objects. But then, what is an object?

Simply put, an object is a collection of methods (functions) that act on data (variables) which are also objects. The blueprint for these objects is a class.

Consider a class a sketch or a prototype that has all the details about an object. If your program were a car, a class would contain all the details about the design, the chassis, where tires are, and what the windshield is made of. It would be impossible to build a car without a class defining it. The car is the object.

Just as many cars can be built based on the prototype, we can create many objects from a class. We can also call an object an instance of a class, and the process by which it is created is called instantiation.

Defining a Class

Classes are defined using the keyword class. Just like a function, a class should have a documentation string (docstring) that briefly explains what the class is and what it does. While the docstring is not mandatory, it is a good practice to have it. Here is a simple definition of a class called NewClass:

```
class NewClass:
    #This is the docstring of the class NewClass that we
    #Just created. Our program now has a new class
    pass
```

When you create a new class, a new local namespace that defines all its attributes is created. Attributes in this case may include functions and data structures. In it, it will contain special attributes that start with ___ (double underscores), like ___doc___, that defines the docstring of the class.

When a class is defined, a new class object with the same name is created. The new class object is what we can use to access the different attributes and to instantiate the new objects of our new class.

Creating a New Class

```
class NewClass:
    #This is our first class. What it does
    #is display a string text and a value of
    #variable name
    name = str(input("Enter your name: "))
    def greeting (name):
        print ("Hello", name)


print (NewClass.name)
print (NewClass.greeting(NewClass.name))
print (NewClass.__doc__)
```

What does your console display when you run the script?

Creating an Object

So far, we have learned that we can access the different attributes of a class using the class objects. We can use these objects to also instantiate new instances of that class using a procedure a lot similar to calling a function.

```
MyObject = NewClass()
```

In the example above, a new instance object called MyObject is created. This object can be used to access the attributes of the class NewClass using the class name as a prefix.

The attributes in this case may include methods and variables. The methods of an object are the corresponding functions of a class meaning that any class attribute function object defines the methods for objects in that class.

For instance, because NewClass.greeting is a function object and an attribute of NewClass, MyObject.greeting will be a method object.

Creating an object:

```
class NewClass:
    #This is our first class. What it does
    #is display a string text and a value of
    #variable name
    name = str(input("Enter your name: "))
    def greeting (name):
        print ("Hello", name)

MyObject = NewClass() #Creates a new NewClass object
print (NewClass.greeting)
print (MyObject.greeting)
MyObject.greeting() # Calling function greeting()
```

The name parameter is within the function definition of the class, but we called the method using the statement MyObject.greeting() without specifying any arguments and it still worked. This is because when an object calls a method defined within it, the object itself passes as the first argument. Therefore, in this case, MyObject.greeting() translates to NewClass.greeting(MyObject).

Generally speaking, when you call a method with a list of x arguments, it is the same as calling the corresponding function using an argument list created when the method's object is inserted before the first argument.

As a result, the first function argument in a class needs to be the object itself. In Python, this is typically called self but it can be assigned any other name. It is important to understand class objects, instance objects, function objects, and method objects and what sets them all apart.

Constructors

In Python, the __init__() function is special because it is called when a new object of its class is instantiated. This object is also called a constructor because it is used to initialize all variables.

Constructors

```
class ComplexNumbers:
    def __init__(self, x = 0, y = 0):
        self.real = x
        self.imagined = y
    def getNumbers(self):
        print ("Complex numbers are: {0}+{1}j".format(self.real,
self.imagined))


Object1 = ComplexNumbers(2, 3) #Creates a new ComplexNumbers object
Object1.getNumbers() #Calls getNumbers() function
Object2 = ComplexNumbers(10) #Creates another ComplexNumbers object
Object2.attr = 20 #Creates a new attribute 'attr'
print((Object2.real, Object2.imagined, Object2.attr))
Object1.attr #Generates an error because c1 object doesn't have attrib-
ute 'attr'
```

In the above exercise, we have defined a new class that represents complex numbers. We have defined two functions, the __init__() function that initializes the variables and the getNumbers() function to properly display the numbers.

Note that the attributes of the objects in the exercise are created on the fly. For instance, the new attribute attr for Object2 was created but one for Object1 was not (hence the error).

Deleting Attributes and Objects

You can delete the attributes of an object or even the object itself at any time using the statement del.

Deleting Attributes and Objects

```
class ComplexNumbers:
    def __init__(self, x = 0, y = 0):
        self.real = x
        self.imagined = y
    def getNumbers(self):
        print ("Complex numbers are: {0}+{1}j".format(self.real,
self.imagined))
Object1 = ComplexNumbers(2, 3) #Creates a new ComplexNumbers object
Object1.getNumbers() #Calls getNumbers() function
Object2 = ComplexNumbers(10) #Creates another ComplexNumbers object
Object2.attr = 20 #Creates a new attribute 'attr'
print ((Object2.real, Object2.imagined, Object2.attr))
del ComplexNumbers.getNumbers
Object1.getNumbers()
```

The error you get when you run the script shows that the attribute getNumbers() has been deleted. Note, however, that since a new instance is created in memory when a new instance of the object is created, the object may continue to exist in memory even after it is deleted until the garbage collector automatically destroys unreferenced objects.

Chapter 17: Inheritance and Polymorphism

In Python, a class is defined using the keyword Class, the same way a function is defined with the keyword def. Therefore, if we were to define a class called ClassName, our syntax would look like this:

```
class ClassName:
    "Class Documentation String"
    Class_Suite
```

In this syntax, the keyword class is used to define a new class, followed by the class name ClassName, and a colon. The class documentation string is essentially a definition or description of the class. The Class_Suite is representative of the entirety of the defining class members, component statements, functions, and data attributes of the class.

Since a class is used to create objects, it is best seen as a way to add consistency to programs created in Python so that they are cleaner, more efficient, and most importantly, functional. To create a class that can be instantiated anywhere in your code, it must be defined at a module's top-level.

Creating a Class in Python

Now that we are familiar with the syntax for creating a class in Python, we'll introduce a class example called Dog.

```
class Dog:
    "Dog class"
    var1 = "Bark"
    var2 = "Jump"
```

Class Declaration and Definition

In Python 3, there is no difference between class declaration and class definition. This is because the two occur simultaneously. Class definition follows declaration and documentation string as demonstrated in our example.

Class Methods and Attributes

A class, defined and created, is not complete unless it has some functionality. Functionalities in a class are defined by setting their attributes, which are best seen as containers for functions and data related to those attributes.

Class attributes include data members like variables and instance variables and methods found using the dot notation. Here are their definitions:

- Class variable: A variable shared by all the class instances and objects.

- Instance variable: A variable unique to an instance of a class. It is typically defined within a method and will only be applicable to the instance of that class.
- Method: Also called a function, a method is defined in a class and defines the behavior of an object.

_ Class Attributes

A class attribute is a functional element that belongs to another object and is accessed via dotted-attribute notation. In Python, complex numbers have data attributes while lists and dictionaries have functional attributes. When you access an attribute, you can also access an object that may have attributes of its own. Class attributes are linked to the classes in which they are defined. The most commonly used objects in OOP are instance objects. Instance data attributes are the primary data attributes that are used. You'll find most use for class data attributes when you require a data type, which does not need any instances.

_ Class Data Attributes

Data attributes are the class variables that are defined by the programmer. They can be used like any other variable when creating the class. Methods can update them within the class. Programmers know these types of attributes better as static members, class variables, or static data. They represent data tied to the class object they belong to and are independent of any class instances.

Example of using class data attributes (xyz):

```
class ABC:
    def __init__(self):
        self.xyz = 10
        self.xyz = self.xyz + 1
print(ABC().xyz)
```

The output of this example code will be 11.

_ Python Class Inheritance

Inheritance is a feature in object-oriented programming that allows a class to inherit methods and attributes from a parent class, also referred to as a base class. This is a very handy feature in programming as it allows the programmer to create a suite of functionality for a single class and then pass them on to sub-classes or child classes. As a result, the program will be able to create new and even overwrite existing functionalities in a child class without affecting the functionality of the parent class.

The sub-classes that inheritance creates will feature the specializations of the parent classes. There are four types of inheritances in Python: single, multilevel, hierarchical, and multiple inheritances.

Single Inheritance

Programming classes that have no inheritance features can be accurately referred to as object-based programming. The program, when run, should create new abstract data types, each with its own operations. However, what separates object-oriented programming from object-based programming is inheritance. Single inheritance is when a class or subclass inherits methods and attributes from one parent class.

Multiple Inheritance

In multiple inheritance, a child class or subclass inherits methods and attributes from multiple classes. For instance, a class C can inherit the features of both class A and B, in the same way that a child inherits the characteristics of both the mother and father. In some cases, a child class can inherit the features and functionalities of more than two parent classes.

There is no limit to the number of parent classes from which a child class can inherit methods and attributes. Note that while multiple inheritances is best known to reduce program redundancy, it may also introduce a higher level of complexity and ambiguity to the program and must be properly thought out during program design before implementation.

Multilevel Inheritance

We have already established that it is possible for a class in Python to inherit features of multiple parent classes. When a class inherits the methods and functions of other classes that also inherit them from other classes, the process is known as multilevel inheritance. Like in C++ and other object-oriented programming languages, Python allows for multilevel inheritance implemented at any depth.

Hierarchical Inheritance

A hierarchical inheritance occurs when more than one class is derived from a single parent or base class. The features inherited by the sub-class or the child class are included in the parent class. What sets hierarchical inheritance apart from a multi-level inheritance is the order in which the relationship between the classes is established. In multilevel inheritance, the order can be haphazard and parent classes can inherit features from previous child classes.

Why is Inheritance Useful in Python Programming?

Inheritance is a very handy feature of object-oriented programming because it allows a programmer to easily adhere to one of software development's most important rules: Don't Repeat Yourself (DRY). Simply put, implementing class inheritance in your programs is the most efficient way to get more done with fewer lines of code and less repetition.

Inheritance will also compel you to pay closer attention to the design phase of programming to ensure that you write a program code that is clean, minimalist, and effective.

Another use of inheritance is adding functionality to various sections of your program.

Inheritance Example

In Python, adding functionality is done by deriving classes. Let's say we have class called SportsCar:

```
class Vehicle(object):
    def __init__(self, makeAndModel, prodYear, airConditioning):
        self.makeAndModel = makeAndModel
        self.prodYear = prodYear
        self.airConditioning = airConditioning
        self.doors = 4
    def honk(self):
        print("%s says: Honk! Honk!" % self.makeAndModel)
```

Now, below that, create a new class called SportsCar, but instead of deriving
object, we're going to derive from Vehicle:

```
class SportsCar(Vehicle):
    def __init__(self, makeAndModel, prodYear, airConditioning):
        self.makeAndModel = makeAndModel
        self.prodYear = prodYear
        self.airConditioning = airConditioning
        self.doors = 4
```

Leave out the honk function, we only need the constructor function here.
Now declare a sports car. I'm just going to go with the Ferrari:

```
ferrari = SportsCar("Ferrari Laferrari", 2016, True)
```

Now test this by calling

```
ferrari.honk()
```

and then saving and running. It should go off without a hitch. Why is this? This is because the notion of inheritance says that a child class derives functions and class variables from a parent class. Easy enough concept to grasp. The next one is a little tougher.

Class Polymorphism and Abstraction

In Computer Science, polymorphism and abstraction are advanced programming features that extend the application and usefulness of inheritance.

Polymorphism means that should class Y inherit from class X, it does not necessarily have to inherit everything from that class. It can implement some of the inherited methods and attributes differently. Python, being implicitly polymorphic, can overload operators to grant them the desired behavior based on individual contexts. The idea of polymorphism is that the same process can be performed in different ways depending upon the needs of the situation. This can be done in two different ways in Python: *method overloading* and *method overriding*.

Method overloading is defining the same function twice with different arguments. For example, we could give two different initializer functions to our Vehicle class. Right now, it just assumes a vehicle has 4 doors. If we wanted to specifically say how many doors a car had, we could make a new initializer function below our current one with an added *doors* argument, like so (the newer one is on the bottom):

```
def __init__(self, makeAndModel, prodYear, airConditioning):
    self.makeAndModel = makeAndModel
    self.prodYear = prodYear
    self.airConditioning = airConditioning
    self.doors = 4
def __init__(self, makeAndModel, prodYear, airConditioning, doors):
    self.makeAndModel = makeAndModel
    self.prodYear = prodYear
    self.airConditioning = airConditioning
    self.doors = doors
```

Now, when creating an instance of the Vehicle class, one can *choose* whether they define the number of doors or not. If they don't, the number of doors is assumed to be 4. *Method overriding* is when a child class *overrides* a parent class's function with its code. To illustrate, create another class which extends Vehicle called Moped. Set the doors to 0, because that's absurd, and set air conditioning to false. The only relevant arguments are make/model and production year. It should look like this:

```
class Moped(Vehicle):
    def __init__(self, makeAndModel, prodYear):
        self.makeAndModel = makeAndModel
        self.prodYear = prodYear
        self.airConditioning = False
        self.doors = 0
```

Now, if we made an instance of the Moped class and called the honk() method, it would honk. But it is common knowledge that mopeds don't honk, they beep. So let's override the parent class's honk method with our own. This is super simple. We just redefine the function in the child class:

```
def honk(self):
    print("%s says: Beep! Beep!" % self.makeAndModel)
```

I'm part of the 299,000,000 Americans who couldn't name a make and model of moped if their life depended on it, but you can test out if this works for yourself but declaring an instance of the Moped class and trying it out.

Abstraction

Abstraction is generally a net positive for a large number of applications that are being written today, and there's a reason Python and other object-oriented programming languages are incredibly popular. Abstraction is the process of simplifying complex realities by modeling classes to handle specific problems. An abstract class cannot be instantiated and you can neither create class instances nor objects for them. Abstract classes are designed to inherit all or only specific features from a base class. Abstraction innately makes the language easier to understand, read, and learn. Though it makes the language a tad bit less powerful by taking away some of the power that the user has over the entire computer architecture, this is traded instead for the ability to program quickly and efficiently in the language, not wasting time dealing with trivialities like memory addresses or things of the like. These apply in Python because, well, it's incredibly simple. You can't get down into the nitty-gritty of the computer, or do much with memory allocation or even specifically allocate an array size too easily, but this is a tradeoff for amazing readability, a highly secure language in a highly secure environment, and ease of use with programming. Compare the following snippet of code from C:

```c
#include <stdio.h>
int main(void) {
    printf("hello world");
    return 0;
}
```

to the Python code for doing the same:

```python
print("hello world")
# That's it. That's all there is to it.
```

Encapsulation

The last major concept in object-oriented programming is that of encapsulation. This one's the easiest to explain. This is the notion that common data should be put together, and that code should be modular. I'm not going to spend long explaining this because it's a super simple concept. The entire notion of classes is as concise of an example as you can get for encapsulation: Common traits and methods are bonded together under one cohesive structure, making it super easy to create things of the sort without having to create a ton of super-specific variables for every instance. Well, there we go.

Conclusion

Programming isn't just about getting a PC to get things done. It is tied in with cmposing code that is helpful to people. Great programming is saddling complexity by composing code that rhymes with our instincts. Great code will be code that we can use with a negligible amount of setting.

The most important thing for you to do is to practice programming in Python. If you have read until here then you have already absorbed quite much. You need to practice all the things you have learned to make sure you consolidate that knowledge (i.e. make it stick).

Knowledge is useless without application. Learning how to program without actual programming will only waste the time you invested here. It is like learning how to ride a bike by reading books or articles about it—that will never be enough! You need to ride a bike to learn how to ride a bike.

Also, make sure to familiarize yourself with useful resources you can easily refer to when you need help. There are two obvious ones: Python's documentation, Stack Exchange.

During your programming journey, you will encounter seemingly impossible problems. During those times, never hesitate to reach out for help.

Get Your Free Gifts

To further complement your preparation and help you accelerate your learning process we are giving you free access to 3 powerful booklets

☑ **FREE eBooklet #1:** Mindset Secrets for Developers

☑ **FREE eBooklet #2:** Basic Coding Interview Questions

☑ **FREE eBooklet #3:** Time Management Principles

→ **To get them scan the following QR Code**

Or go to

https://bigrocksgroup.com/codeonepublishing/

Made in the USA
Coppell, TX
08 December 2022